"Sedley and Coyne are two experts who have written a terrific guide for teens with obsessive-compulsive disorder (OCD). They walk the reader through how to understand obsessions and compulsions, and how to use exposure and response prevention (ERP) and acceptance-based strategies to better manage these unpleasant experiences. What's unique about this book is how well the authors speak to their young readers; engaging them with personal accounts of OCD and abundant illustrations. If your teen with OCD is having difficulty engaging with treatment, this is the book for them!"

—Jonathan Abramowitz, PhD, professor in the department of psychology at The University of North Carolina at Chapel Hill, and author of *Getting Over OCD*

"*Stuff That's Loud* is a book I wish teen me had. It's written in a comforting and encouraging way by clinicians that get OCD, and its treatment. But more than this, it's a book about exploration and invention of the life you want to live. If you are a teen with this book in your hands, I hope it helps you work through OCD and create the life you want, filled with all the fun, meaning, and adventure possible."

—Stuart Ralph, author of *The OCD Stories*

"In some ways, the fundamentals of recovering from OCD have not changed. You face the things you fear and resist engaging in compulsions. What has changed, however, is the way in which many therapists conceptualize, motivate, and guide individuals through this process. Sedley and Coyne represent a new generation of therapists who have infused the recovery process with concepts like resiliency, willingness, and psychological flexibility. Most importantly, they challenge us to live according to our values, rather than the dictates of our negative emotions and thoughts. And they do so in an informative and engaging way."

—C. Alec Pollard, PhD, director of the Center for OCD and Anxiety-Related Disorders at Saint Louis Behavioral Medicine Institute; and professor emeritus of family and community medicine at Saint Louis University School of Medicine

"Hearing and telling stories is at the heart of being human. Sometimes we tell a story that eases a friend's pain, or at least lets them know they are not alone. Sometimes we hear a story, and in it, we hear a way forward. Ben and Lisa bring together many stories of actual teens who have struggled with OCD. These are real people who have made the journey and are continuing to make the journey. They share their stories in the hope that you will join them on the road. There is a deep kindness in this book and a way forward. If you are weary of the struggle, read this book. Maybe in its pages you will find some rest, fellowship, and a road map to meaning and purpose."

—**Kelly G. Wilson, PhD**, professor emeritus in the department of psychology at the University of Mississippi, and author of *Mindfulness for Two* and *Things Might Go Terribly, Horribly Wrong*

"Coyne and Sedley have come up with some 'stuff that's great' for teens grappling with OCD. *Stuff That's Loud* offers its readers easy-to-understand therapeutic concepts in a tone that is both credible and compassionate. The book acknowledges how painful unwanted thoughts and rituals can be, but rather than dwell on this, the authors consistently bring the reader back to a focus on the wonderful potential teens have when they learn to relate to their OCD differently."

—**Jon Hershfield, MFT**, author of *Overcoming Harm OCD* and *When a Family Member Has OCD*

"Helping a teenager manage OCD isn't easy. There just aren't many resources to help them understand OCD in a relatable way. *Stuff That's Loud* successfully demystifies OCD, clues kids into what's going on with their brains, and, most importantly, helps them find a way to fight back. The book is everything OCD hates: Insightful. Supportive. Challenging. Encouraging. I highly recommend it."

—**Chris Baier**, parent of a teen with OCD, and producer of the award-winning *UNSTUCK*

CONTENTS

⏸ Intro

IT MIGHT SEEM OUTLANDISH for me to brazenly declare that 1950s rock and roll never happened, but music bizzers had reason to suspect a mass hallucination. The phrase circulated because DJ Alan Freed needed a replacement name for his New York radio show in 1954, and *rocking and rolling* stood for sex in the Black-identified R&B songs he played to white teens. That usage got reinforcement when Bill Haley and His Comets' "Rock Around the Clock" featured to start the film *Blackboard Jungle* the next year. Rock and roll, the story goes, was dead at the end of the 1950s: Elvis Presley was in the army, Little Richard a Christian, Chuck Berry in jail, Buddy Holly and Ritchie Valens dead in a plane crash, Jerry Lee Lewis ostracized, Freed charged with payola, the whole sick crew replaced by clean-cut kids like Fabian on television's *American Bandstand*. Really, though, the issue was that, unlike rhythm and blues and country and western at the time, or rock starting only in the late 1960s, rock and roll had no infrastructure. Even radio stations that played it were called Top 40, not what the punk Ramones later fantasized: rock and roll radio.

Still, baby boomers could continue to believe that rock and roll would stand, to sanctify it, because one thing made its alchemy complete: the single. The great schism that divorced seven-inch 45 RPM vinyl singles from twelve-inch 33.3 RPM LPs in the post–World War II era, where everything had once been ten-inch 78 RPM shellac, made the smaller format a bastion of youth music and working-class genres like the electric blues of R&B and the electric country of honkytonk. In the familiar histories of rock and roll, told by *Rolling Stone* and the Rock and Roll Hall of Fame, that created a revolution—youth, Black, and southern styles colliding with a thunderclap.

More adroit interpreters have noted how that thunderclap, caterwauling guitar solos and soaring, doubled-up *whooo*s, made it onto singles in the first place: a new technology, magnetic recording, allowed multiple takes, multitracking, edits, tricks to fashion records into minimovies. They were now a world unto themselves, alternative realities. Schizophonia, cutting sounds from sources, had always been an aspect of recording. But where the previous innovation, electrical recording, worked against that, welcoming the intimacy of a crooned breath, a cool sax, instead of still earlier acoustic recording's windy bellow, magnetic recordings were theatrical and alienating again: electrified, blaring, amateuristic—unidentifiable freaky objects.

Sixty-plus years later, rock and roll has spawned not only a hall for canonization but a connected Cleveland archive for research. YouTube, Spotify, Bear Family box sets, and the like offer performance repositories. In other ways, we're just beginning to reckon with what took place in the moment of "Maybellene" and "Tutti Frutti," able to consider race, sexuality, and other elements rarely dissected in their day beyond the outcries of conservatives and jazz fans. Back then, a lot couldn't be candidly addressed, and the most fervent listeners were too young to articulate their passions. Anyway, the rock and roll records that became all but supernatural to those listeners clearly, blazingly, worked their magic just fine whatever the hell they were.

"Hound Dog" waits for us at this intersection of revisionism and identity politics. Most listeners first heard Elvis Presley's version, recorded in 1956 and topping the pop, R&B, and country charts. But R&B fans knew it was a cover: Willie Mae "Big Mama" Thornton's 1953 single had been a giant hit in that fledgling format, with no attempt made at crossover. A white guy's lift of a Black woman's anthem: What could better represent the outright appropriation that cultural studies scholar Eric Lott has called "love and theft"?[1] To reply, defensively, that the song's writers were white, along with some of the musicians playing on it, only defers the issue— these were all Black music admirers/appropriators, too.

Boomers cherished the Elvis "Hound Dog" as a kind of Frosted Flake: it tasted great and revved them up, but eventually their diet became more adult. Bob Dylan, John Lennon, Keith Richards, and the other new guys kept the King outside their group chat, revering him from a distance as he got fat in Graceland, then died at forty-two in 1977. By this point, rock and roll itself was getting its first debunking: "No Elvis, Beatles, or the Rolling Stones in 1977," the Clash sang in their punk manifesto "1977." For *London Calling*, their cover image sarcastically reworked a Presley cover—instead of the 1950s rocker letting loose as his guitar, voice, and body erupted, you saw Paul Simonon in hunchbacked posture, getting set to smash his bass. That became canon, too—rituals of what Kurt Cobain, in 1991's "Smells Like Teen Spirit," called, over and over, "a denial."

Only punk hadn't gone far enough. In 2021 *Rolling Stone* released its first list in a generation of "The 500 Greatest Songs of All Time." A document of critical consensus, it gives this book a useful hook. In one of the greatest shifts, Presley's "Hound Dog," number 19 in the 2004 version (his highest ranking), disappeared altogether in 2021, replaced by Thornton's "Hound Dog" in the bottom half, at 318.[2] Canon upending is a given in our moment. Much important music writing does what this new list does: change the players, retell the history from their perspective, center what was once left to the margins.

But I'm thinking about what happens to marginalize something that was once central. For a time, my formative lifetime, marginalizing the center was just a wordy way of being a punk rocker. You can see the evidence in that 2004 *Rolling Stone* list, where the only "newer" songs sharing space in the top 20 with Elvis, Beatles, Dylan, Stones, Chuck Berry, Ray Charles, and Marvin Gaye were the punk denial anthems: the Clash's "London Calling" and Nirvana's "Smells Like Teen Spirit."

The expurgation of Elvis is something else, denial in far more sweeping terms. It recasts who gets to rock. And it changes what we value in noise and rebellion. Rock and roll's foundational narrative canonized something aggressive and life-altering shooting out of those 1950s singles, whose impact took decades to absorb and whose spirit resisted appropriation. Many loved "Hound Dog" in part as a song that helped drive Patti Page's tame, mainstream "(How Much Is) That Doggie in the Window," and all that went with it, off their planet. That take is now fading: the question is how much will shift in the process. At this point, "Hound Dog" stands in for every question that has ever been raised about musical thievery and reconstituted whiteness.

For the first rock and rollers, it courts charges of cliché to note, "Hound Dog" served as evidence, the proof of concept that a young John Lennon in Liverpool could clutch to heart and begin life anew as a Beatle. Rock criticism proved no less reverent, from Nik Cohn's UK defense of Presley's pop appeal against rock seriousness to the "Presliad" finale of Greil Marcus's foundational US account, *Mystery Train*, which embraced the King, from all-out rock to squalid schlock, as a story worthy of America's contradictions. Presley's cover of Thornton couldn't be racist, Marcus argued, because the song's origins were so mongrel to begin with. Anyhow, he thought Presley's version was better; it demanded more. "We will never agree on anything as we agreed on Elvis," Lester Bangs wrote in Presley's *Village Voice* obituary.[3]

But he was writing in the past tense, about the spirit of 1956. Black listeners had rejected Presley not long after he triumphed, pushed away in part by a made-up story that he'd said they should shine his shoes and buy his records, but ultimately by the obvious contrast between his integrated repertoire and segregated legacy. Alice Walker's 1981 short story "Nineteen Fifty-Five" was a sharp note of Black dissent, with a protagonist modeled on Presley begging a protagonist modeled on Thornton to explain what his big hit song was about. Tyina Steptoe's 2018 article "Big Mama Thornton, Little Richard, and the Queer Roots of Rock 'n' Roll" enfolded several layers of revisionism: a Black scholar putting Black artists at the core of rock and roll history—and queer Black performance at that. (A photo of Steptoe's grandfather with Thornton ran with the piece: Why should white boomers be the only protagonists in the arena of cultural memory?) Thornton was "a three-hundred-pound, twenty-six-year-old black woman who dressed in suits and ties," and her look and sound, like Richard's, displayed a "commitment to gender nonconformity and a rejection of heteronormativity." Her spirit, abstracted for 1950s standards in ways not required of earlier classic blues singer Ma Rainey, was rock and roll's spirit. The appropriation by Elvis, Steptoe made clear via Jack Halberstam (author of *Female Masculinity*), was from queer to straight as much as Black to white.[4]

Maureen Mahon's prizewinning *Black Diamond Queens* centered on Black women rockers from Thornton to Tina Turner.

Did Thornton author "Hound Dog"? At least, Presley "picked up on her refusals." Her command. "He makes a million and all this jive because his face is different from mine," Mahon noted that Thornton had said. And if you thought about it, Mahon wrote, contrasted with Thornton's spirited rebuke of a scoundrel man, "Presley's version of the song didn't make sense": Who was the dog? In Mahon's more expansive accounting, "if we listen, we can hear a line of descent from Thornton to Elvis Presley and Janis Joplin on through to Robert Plant, Axl Rose, Kurt Cobain, Jack White, and Brittany Howard." Fittingly, Mahon ends with Howard, like Thornton a child of Alabama but able—in our era, where the Willie Mae Rock Camp named for Thornton teaches girls to play, sing, and write—to be unabashedly a rock star. By the way, Jerry Leiber and Mike Stoller said in their joint memoir that they preferred Thornton's version to Presley's. When I teach the two recordings in classes, I get the sense my students do, too.[5]

Can a book, in the 2020s, accept this history, accept the backlash to this history, then ask what remains of the original rock and roll allure that pulled so many into records, singles especially, in the first place? "Hound Dog" remains well suited for the mission: seemingly every iteration of music writing since 1956 has confronted its arc. And the Presley version has hardly disappeared: it reached over 180 million plays on Spotify circa the much-touted summer 2022 biopic, *Elvis*, directed by Baz Luhrmann. As with that streaming service, we now have tools for investigating "Hound Dog" that would have been hard for earlier listeners and writers to replicate. We can repeatedly watch the television performances by Presley that flew past and were gone, even as they made his hips a national controversy and preceded the recording of the song.

For all this increased ease of access, a belabored hesitancy has settled in over how to view the white man rocking. The rough music that Marcus heard as overturning restraints—the limits a country singer from a working-class background like Hank Williams epitomized but former truck driver Presley threw off—resounds now like Tea Party, Trump, and SEC football populism. Our pop histories don't start with rock and roll these days or imagine rural blues streaming into some great river of sound. They confront blackface minstrelsy, northern whites in the 1830s moment of white male Jacksonian democracy putting on a crude "southern" "Blackness" to scream at the new bourgeoisie. Lott's *Love and Theft* embedded these questions of racial appropriation in the full arc of US history, noting, "Its modern resonance is articulated in white guitarist Scotty Moore's remark to Elvis Presley at one of the recording sessions in which Elvis first found his voice: '*Damn*, n****r!'"[6]

After the session that produced the recording of "Hound Dog" in thirty-one takes, Presley requested an acetate, so he could better study the sound that had come out of him. He wasn't playing "Hound Dog" for laughs anymore, nor, as Thornton had, grooving on it. What had he locked onto instead? It's not clear from the twenty-one years that followed, half his life, that Presley ever

"Combining Ben Sedley's approach to helping teens with Lisa Coyne's skill in working with adolescents with OCD results in a great book. The skills taught in this book will help at any stage of the struggle with OCD. Every teen struggling with OCD will benefit from their work."

—**Michael Twohig, PhD**, professor in the department of psychology at Utah State University

"Much has been written about how to develop resilience in young adults. The problem in the past is there has been an inadequate framework and insufficient science to back up the claims. It is hard to teach children and teenagers about emotional difficulties without triggering their interest, unleashing a variety of effective strategies (because nothing works for everyone), and offering empathy and guidance on how to apply these strategies to optimize their day-to-day lives. This short, compelling book is a pleasure to read, and I suspect even skeptical readers will feel the same way. The exquisite illustrations; the direct communication to the reader; the clear and concrete suggestions and experiments. I suspect many people will be helped by reading and rereading these pages."

—**Todd B. Kashdan, PhD**, professor in the department of psychology at George Mason University, and coauthor of *The Upside of Your Dark Side*

"*Stuff That's Loud* is hands-down the best self-help I have seen on OCD. If you're a teen, inside these pages you'll find a way to make your life bigger than OCD. If you're a professional, you'll find the tools and language that will help you guide young people out of the spiral of OCD. And if you're a parent, you'll find the language to help you support your teen's journey into a life well lived."

—**Louise Hayes, PhD**, clinical psychologist, and coauthor of *The Thriving Adolescent*

"Lisa Coyne and Ben Sedley have written an irreverent, compassionate, and informative book for any teen struggling with OCD. It's a pleasure to read, and it's grounded in ERP, the most effective treatment we have for treating OCD. I would recommend this to anyone who wants to get to know how they spiral, and how to get out."

—Matthew S. Boone, LCSW, editor of *Mindfulness and Acceptance in Social Work*

"If you're a teen with OCD, reading *Stuff That's Loud* is like hanging out with a trusted best friend: someone who's not only been there, done that, but is hip and cool, completely gets you and your struggles, and shares things in a way that you actually find useful. Lisa and Ben have created an empowering and engaging guide that will help teens focus not on what OCD cares about, but what matters to them. Every teen with OCD needs this book!"

—Shala Nicely, author of *Is Fred in the Refrigerator?*

STUFF THAT'S LOUD

a teen's guide to unspiraling when ocd gets noisy

BEN SEDLEY | LISA COYNE

Instant Help Books

An Imprint of New Harbinger Publications, Inc.

Publisher's Note

Distributed in Canada by Raincoast Books

Copyright © 2020 by Ben Sedley
    Instant Help Books
    An imprint of New Harbinger Publications, Inc.
    5674 Shattuck Avenue
    Oakland, CA 94609
    www.newharbinger.com

Lines from *Turtles All the Way Down* by John Green, copyright © 2017 by John Green. Used by permission of Penguin Random House LLC.

When Things Fall Apart: Heart Advice for Difficult Times by Pema Chödrön, pp. 44-45. Copyright © 1997 by Pema Chödrön. Reprinted by arrangement with The Permissions Company LLC on behalf of Shambhala Publications, Inc., Boulder, Colorado, www.shambhala.com.

Cover design by Amy Shoup

Illustrations by Kalos Chan

Book design by Wonderbird Photography & Design Studio (Catherine Adam)

Library of Congress Cataloging-in-Publication Data on file

25   24   23

10   9   8   7   6   5   4   3

THE UNOFFICIAL BEGINNING

Welcome to the unofficial beginning of *Stuff That's Loud*.

I find it hard to listen to someone I don't know so I'm going to start off by introducing myself. I am an eighteen-year-old boy who has just entered university. Now, depending on who you are, eighteen may sound either really old, really young, or just right. I'm not an accomplished author, researcher, or doctor, but I am someone you might be able to relate to.

When I was fourteen years old, the anxiety and OCD I had been struggling with for years came to a peak. I won't bore you with the details, but I was in pretty bad shape. I was miserable, I barely left the house, and on top of that, I was making my family miserable as well. The stuff that's loud in my head was all I ever focused on. For the longest time, I didn't even want treatment for my condition. Not because I didn't want to get better, but for the opposite reason. I wanted to get better, but I wanted to be sure that I was the one who made it happen. I didn't want any therapist to "fix" me. The way I saw it, this was my struggle, and if I could overcome this on my own, I could live the rest of my life knowing that I could do anything.

Well, I was half-right and half-wrong. This was one of the biggest struggles I'd ever faced, and overcoming it was invaluable in shaping the person I am today. But I was wrong to think that anyone could "fix" me. Whether it's a therapist, medicine, or even a book like this one, there is no magic that is going to "fix" you. If your struggle is a battle, then those are your weapons. All anyone or anything can do is give you weapons and strategies to fight your battle with. But in the end, you are the only one who can make a difference.

You may have mixed feelings about hearing this. I know I've had moments when all I wanted was for somebody to wave a magic wand over my head and make everything all right. I just wanted to be better and for the noise in my head to be silenced. I'd do anything to make it happen. I'm sorry to tell you that it's not likely to work out like that. You can choose to see this as a bad thing, or you can see it as a great opportunity. There are many problems in this world and struggles in life that, no matter how hard we try, we may never make a difference in. But this is not one of those. **I can personally tell you that you, and you alone, have the power to shape what the rest of your life will look like.** Life has presented you with an opportunity to gain experience that others may not get until much later in their lives. Although it may be hard to feel this way at the moment, one day you might even think you were lucky to have come face-to-face with the stuff that's loud.

—Ethan Ganster, May 2019

Hey there! I'm a seventeen-year-old girl, and if you hadn't already figured this out, I have OCD. I was lucky enough to be diagnosed at just nine years old, but at the time the diagnosis was no more than more incomprehensible doctor talk. As a young girl and later a teenager playing tug-of-war with my thoughts, what I wanted more than anything was for someone else to make the distress go away. Unlike many kids with similar struggles, I wasn't opposed to treatment. In fact,

I was eager to meet anyone who might lift some of this burden off my back. At the lowest point of my life, I felt paralyzed by these uncontrollable, loud thoughts. Some days, they were so loud that I couldn't get off the floor. I was scared. My family was petrified. I wanted a magic solution to my problems.

It took me years to learn that I had to be the one to make the change; no one else was going to do it for me, because no one else had that ability. If there's one thing you take from this book, I hope that's it: you have the power to make your life better. But it's your choice. I firmly believe that this book will help people with struggles similar to mine. I wish something like this had been around at the beginning of my journey, but I am grateful that it exists now.

I know that words of encouragement will take you only so far. With that in mind, I'll try to keep this brief. If you're experiencing something similar to what I felt, you might not be able to even imagine digging yourself out of this hole. **I'm here to tell you that even if you can't visualize such a change, it's possible. Trust in your ability to choose a life worth living.**

—Shira Folberg, May 2019

The young warrior roused herself and went toward Fear, prostrated three times, and asked, "May I have permission to go into battle with you?"

Fear said, "Thank you for showing me so much respect that you ask permission." Then the young warrior said, "How can I defeat you?"

Fear replied, "My weapons are that I talk fast, and I get very close to your face. Then you get completely unnerved, and you do whatever I say. If you don't do what I tell you, I have no power.

You can listen to me, and you can have respect for me. You can even be convinced by me. But if you don't do what I say, I have no power."

In that way, the student warrior learned how to defeat fear.

—Pema Chödrön
When Things Fall Apart: Heart Advice for Difficult Times

Part One

SPIRALING

Chapter 1

STUFF THAT'S US

Listen to me or something terrible will happen.

Does your mind say stuff like that? Does it say it really loudly?

Do your thoughts and worries spiral and then suck you in?

Do the thoughts show up and make you scared of doing certain things—or not doing things—a particular way?

Are you ever certain something bad will happen?

Do images sneak into your mind and attack you or repulse you or make you worry that you might do something you would hate to do?

Do you ever feel like you need to do things until they feel just right or perfect?

Do you question whether you are okay? Or whether you did something harmful? Or whether life has meaning?

Does not knowing feel terrifying? Is uncertainty intolerable?

Does your mind get stuck doing things over and over, or even just avoiding doing things, or going to places, or being with people, entirely?

Do you worry? Are you scared to tell anyone?

Do you try to hide these worries from other people because you're terrified about what they might think of you?

Do you worry that having these thoughts means something bad about you? Like if you can think it, you could do it? Are you ashamed of the thoughts you have?

Do the worries make you feel alone?

This is the stuff that's loud.

SPOILER ALERT

You're not going crazy (although you might worry that you are).

You're not alone (even though you might feel it).

You can get through this. In fact, you can do more than just get through this. You can live a life full of meaning and healthy relationships and joy.

Right now your mind might be asking "How can you make claims like that when you don't know me, and you haven't heard my loud stuff?" Your mind is right. **We don't know you**. We don't know what your particular thought spirals are, and we don't know which particular sneaky games your thought spirals play on you.

But we do know lots about the stuff that's loud and the tricks it likes to play to make it harder for you to do things you would like to do. **What we offer are ideas and strategies that have helped other people**. These ideas have research behind them to show they are likely to work for you too.

We invite you to be open to these ideas. Try them. Really try them, even the uncomfortable or scary ones. If they help you, then yay. If they're not quite the right fit for you, then keep looking for solutions that help you move toward the life you would like to be living. **Because your life doesn't have to stay stuck** (even when thoughts are loud). And if you are having any doubts about whether the ideas in this book will help (or that anything will help), chances are that worry is one more sneaky trick the stuff that's loud is playing on you.

We're guessing that you're holding this book because you are struggling with loud, unrelenting, worrying thoughts. Your struggle might have been labeled **obsessive compulsive disorder** (OCD), or it may not have been given a name before. We're calling it the **stuff that's loud**.

The stuff that's loud is those thoughts, or feelings, or sensations that are so persistent, intrusive, and terrifying that they occupy your attention, your emotions, and your body. Often other things need to be put on hold until you've done something to calm the loud stuff. Maybe you even have to do those things over and over. These things you do are often called rituals or compulsions and they can take away the anxiety temporarily, but then the anxiety returns and you find yourself having to do the ritual again and again. These rituals might be inside your head, or they might be things that others can see you do. Or maybe you're really good at hiding them (at least some of the time). Or maybe things have gotten so loud that you have opted out of doing anything, because it's been so hard to do stuff over and over, or to try to get things to feel right. If you're like many other people with OCD, you may also feel hopeless and down and trapped by this.

There's you, and there's your OCD. We're going to assume that you wish the stuff that's loud

didn't have such a powerful grip on you. You are ready to find a way to make it go away and stop having so much power over your life. But at the same time, you're terrified of what life would be like without the stuff that's loud being bossy and controlling. It's hard to even imagine a life without it telling you what to do.

Most people around you probably don't get what you're going through. You may have worked really hard to make sure no one finds out about your worries. The stuff that's loud might tell you that it is more likely to become true if you tell someone. You might be incredibly worried that others will think you're crazy if they find out. You might be really ashamed of what you're doing. Because the stuff that's loud tells you to do things and then tells you you're a freak for doing them.

Maybe you have tried to tell people. Maybe they got it or maybe they didn't. Perhaps they told you not to think about such things or not to be so silly. They might have told you that you have a mental illness or that it's not your fault. Maybe they even help you plan your day in such a way that it's easier to do what the stuff that's loud is telling you to do, or they tell you that it's all going to be okay.

Regardless of how others respond, **there are likely times when you feel alone, crazy, broken, or wrong. These thoughts, and the stuff you try to do to quiet them, are very common for people struggling with the stuff that's loud.** In fact they're one of the ways that the stuff that's loud keeps its power.

One of the goals of this book is to let you know that you're not alone and you're certainly not crazy or broken or wrong. In fact, you're part of a tribe.

Did you know …

Anxiety and obsessive compulsive disorders aren't rare. **Approximately 30 percent of teens struggle with anxiety,** and up to 3 percent of teens have OCD, so others you know are trying to live a life with the stuff that's loud. Maybe you're one of the 50 percent of people with OCD who had their first symptoms in childhood, so it's really had time to settle into your mind and get comfortable making you uncomfortable. It is equally common in males and females, and for lots of young people with OCD, other stuff like sadness and anxiety tend to show up along the way too. Teens who struggle with OCD are also more likely to have depression. And the sadness and anxiety can make life even tougher, especially when really dark thoughts show up.

But did you also know …

… just having to deal with the stuff that's loud may have already made you stronger and more resilient. Often in ways you didn't expect or maybe aren't even aware of yet.

Your experiences might be stressful and frustrating and getting in the way of so many parts of your life. But please know, just because you're stuck in a thought spiral, tormented by the stuff that's loud, that doesn't mean there is anything abnormal or unwell about you. We all have different things we struggle with, and this is what you're struggling with at the moment. And it can pass.

All those thoughts that are telling you that there's something wrong with you or that you'll be stuck like this forever or that no one will ever understand what you're going through—all those thoughts are just more stuff that's loud. Sometimes really loud. And sometimes really sneaky and persuasive.

In the next chapter, **Stuff That Spirals**, we're going to meet a range of people who have struggled with the stuff that's loud. Obviously we've changed a few details to protect their privacy, but the experiences and the worries are real. We feel so grateful for all we've learned from the young people who have shared their stories with us.

Then we're going to talk about **Stuff That Makes the Spirals Spirallier**. We know that when the stuff that's loud is at its loudest it can tell you to do rituals or check things or clean things or all sorts of other frustrating messages. It might lead you to develop some strategies that help you feel safer or make the worries less likely to come true. Maybe the stuff that's loud tricks you into avoiding certain places or activities or people. For some people, even leaving home or their bedroom becomes overwhelming or terrifying. It doesn't take long before big painful emotions like shame, self-blame, loneliness, or despair show up. The whole world can feel out of control. The stuff that's loud can really do a number on you.

Next we'll introduce some ideas that can help you unspiral in three steps. First we'll talk about **Curiosity**; you'll notice where you are right now and what it feels like to be looking from this perspective. By doing this, you'll notice other angles too. Then we'll move on to **Willingness**,

where you'll use your curiosity to help take steps toward the life you care about. In **Giving a $#!%**, you'll do more thinking about the people, things, and ideas that matter to you, and that can help with willingness. Finally, the **Flexibility** chapter will discuss ways to practice these three steps anywhere and everywhere.

Near the end of the book we'll talk about **Your Parents, and What to Do with Them**, so that the help they provide actually feels helpful. We'll discuss ways to go about **Building an Army**, finding others who struggle, because you are not alone. We'll also suggest **Other Stuff That Helps**.

This book is intended to be a guide to get you started on the way to unspiraling and finding freedom from OCD. That being said, tackling OCD is best accomplished with a therapist who is knowledgeable about OCD and exposure and response prevention (ERP). If you have a therapist, maybe you and your therapist might even choose to work through this book together. We will also ask you questions throughout the book. You might choose to answer these in your mind, write them in a journal, or discuss them in an OCD community (near where you live or online). However you do this, please slow down, and take your time on our questions. 'Cause if you don't, who will?

YOUR GUIDES

So who's going to come along with you as you experiment with new ways of living with the stuff that's loud?

Ben is a clinical psychologist and the author of *Stuff That Sucks: A Teen's Guide to Accepting What You Can't Change and Committing to What You Can.* He works with teens and adults, many of who are struggling with stuff that's loud or weighed down by shame, self-blame, sadness, or despair. He often wishes his brain would stay on one topic for longer or be a bit quieter from time to time.

Lisa is a clinical psychologist and the founder of the McLean OCD Institute for Children and Adolescents, and an affiliate of Harvard Medical School, and the New England Center for OCD and Anxiety, and is active in the International OCD Foundation. She's the coauthor of *Acceptance and Commitment Therapy: The Clinician's Guide for Supporting Parents*, along with other books and research papers. She spends most days with teens who are struggling with OCD or anxiety, and she also supports their parents. Lisa is a perfectionist, and her mind can be a real jerk about that.

Between chapters we've also included some quotes from young people who have used the ideas we recommend in this book and have come out the other side of OCD.

There is one more guide we'd like you to listen to on this journey. This trip will be rough and spirally and steep at times; the stuff that's loud is sneaky and will do all it can to keep you doing what it tells you. You're going to need lots of support.

Is it okay if we try something now? We invite you to read the instructions, then put the book down and give it a go.

Take a breath. (You'll soon see that many of the things we try will begin with asking you to take a breath.)

Notice as the breath comes in.

And as the breath goes out.

And in your mind's eye, we invite you to think about who you would like to have come along with you on this journey. It can be anyone—someone you know, maybe a friend or family member. It might be a celebrity you've read about or someone from a film or book. Maybe you'd like to choose You from the future, after you've gotten through this, made progress on your journey.

Whoever you've chosen is on your side. They speak to you in a way that is kind, strong, confident, and wise. They're going to come along with you all the way, standing alongside you shoulder to shoulder cheering for you. They'll help you celebrate when you have a good moment, and they'll say something kind but firm when you have an off moment so you can refocus and get back on track. They are your compassionate guide.

Notice what it feels like as you tune in to their voice.

Notice that you're not alone.

Chapter 2

STUFF THAT SPIRALS

You are not alone. You've got us on your team, as well as many others you haven't met yet—more on that later. You've got your own kind, strong, and wise voice you can tune in to.

You are climbing a mountain that others have walked. Let's listen to some of their stories.

SHE WAS STUCK

Daisy was stuck in the same chair, in the same room, for five years. Moving just didn't *feel right*. And it was really the only place she felt was uncontaminated in her house. One by one, her friends drifted away. She kept lots of art supplies—so many she could barely get into her bedroom—because one day, she might become an artist. Keeping all the art supplies meant that a life as an artist would be possible. Getting rid of anything meant closing that door. But becoming an artist felt like a distant dream.

Right now, she was too busy trying to keep herself from getting contaminated, and the rules were tough. She couldn't touch anything, had to keep her hair tied up at all times, could barely use the bathroom, couldn't dress herself, couldn't speak sometimes. She couldn't move. Some days it would take her hours to even pee. Her mom had to do most things for her. It felt like there was no way out.

HIS MIND NEVER RESTED

Years before anyone else even noticed he was struggling, Evan was stuck doing mental rituals. Soon it felt like if he didn't do one of the rituals right, he would die. His mind told him that he would take on qualities of his stepfather that he hated—it was terrifying. If he felt contaminated by his stepfather's voice or presence, it felt like his throat was filling up with sand. It got so bad that his stepfather had to move out of the house. From the moment he woke until he finally fell asleep, Evan was doing rituals or avoiding moving so he could avoid doing rituals. At least when he was asleep he couldn't feel anything for a while.

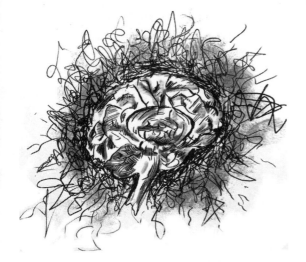

SHE WORRIED SHE WASN'T GETTING IT RIGHT

Mira worried about what she ate. She couldn't stop checking and rechecking in her mind. She lost weight. She felt sick to her stomach. Then she started thinking about her relationships. She worried about the rightness of the emotions she felt toward others. She would constantly check her feelings. Was she really feeling the way she thought she was? Deep down, did she actually hate this person? Did she like that person too much? She exhausted herself by constantly trying to make others happy. Unfortunately, she started to neglect herself in the process. She began to isolate from her friends. She was losing the people and things she cared about most. Was she ever going to get her old life back?

HE HAD TO SAVE THE WORLD

Adam was sure that a huge meteor was going to hit Earth and kill everyone. It was imminent. If he didn't do his rituals just right, his parents and other people would be in grave danger. But it was soooo hard to get the rituals right—sometimes he'd have to do them for hours. He could hide all of this at school, and then he would get home and fall apart.

He'd have to do tapping and stepping and saying protective statements and asking for lots of reassurance for hours and hours. His parents got so mad at him. He was so sad—he was only trying to keep them safe, to keep the world safe, and they just didn't understand. He felt like he was failing, and that would be catastrophic. He didn't know what to do.

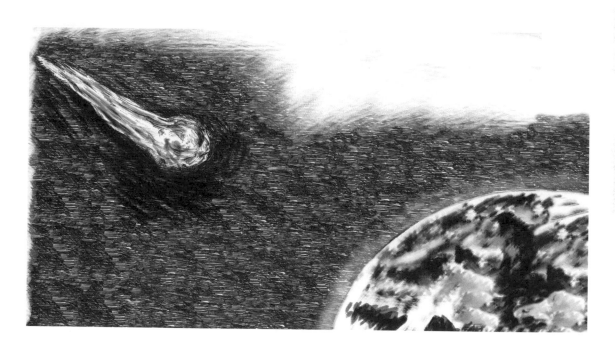

HE THOUGHT, THEREFORE HE WAS, OR WAS HE?

Harry *had* to know whether we really existed. He *felt* alive, but what if he wasn't? What if his feelings were just an illusion, and neither he nor anyone else existed? What if he existed, and *no one else did, and he was all alone*? That was terrifying. How could he know? There was no one to trust. He kept asking his mom for reassurance. He asked her to look stuff up online about the nature of existence—he couldn't bring himself to do it. What if he found out we didn't exist? That would be horrifying—but he had to know. But what if he could never know? He wasn't willing to live in a world where he couldn't know for certain.

HE HAD TO HIDE THE MONSTER

Derrick had terrifying images in his mind all the time. He was convinced he was going crazy. He kept imagining harming little kids … or people around him who he loved. He was terrified he might snap and harm them. If he saw a pen, he thought, "Am I going to stab my friend in the eye?" And then the images would come of him doing it. Was he a murderer? A sociopath? Or schizophrenic—was he losing his mind? How could he know if he was going to act on these thoughts? He was terrified of telling anyone—but if he didn't, did that mean he was trying to hide his true nature? He couldn't figure out a way to protect other people from him. He was so afraid he was a monster.

SHE PRAYED TO BE OKAY

Claudia prayed all the time because she was scared she might have committed a mortal sin. She couldn't get the thought out of her head. Did she do something that was sinful? Sometimes she worried that she had been unkind or had said something hurtful to someone, so she said a little prayer, always the same way, in her head until it felt right. The only problem was, more and more, she couldn't get the "just right" feeling about the prayer. She now had to feel the "right" way in order to say her prayers; otherwise she worried that they wouldn't work—they wouldn't be honest or real. Nighttime was especially hard because she was alone with her thoughts, and they were so, so loud. Some nights it was impossible to sleep.

SHE HAD TO MAKE EVERYTHING PERFECT

At school, Mona lived from test to test. She needed perfect scores on her tests, perfect grades on her papers. All of them, every time, perfect. She had to rehearse everything she was learning in her mind over and over again, until it felt just right. Otherwise she couldn't be sure it would be perfect. She checked with teachers incessantly to make sure she knew what she was supposed to; she showed them multiple drafts of her papers—so many that her teachers started to look annoyed and say that they didn't have any more time to meet. She didn't have time for friends or sports or anything else. Her mind berated her all the time. It told her she was stupid, that she needed to work harder, that anything less than a perfect grade made her worthless. "I need this voice in my head in order to achieve," she told herself. There was no other option. And yet ... she was exhausted. She tried not to think about all the friends she had lost. That type of life just wasn't for her ... but part of her was so very sad that she had to make everything perfect ... that she worried so much about it.

HE COULDN'T KNOW FOR SURE

Noah couldn't keep the images out of his mind, and he didn't know what they meant. It was horrible—every time his eyes fell on another boy … he saw himself doing sexual things to him … he felt a jolt of terror. He had friends who had described their struggle coming out as gay. They knew they were gay but weren't sure how to tell people. That wasn't Noah's struggle. He didn't have a problem with gay people; however he knew he wasn't gay himself. So what did the images mean? If he wasn't gay, why did these pictures keep popping up? He felt more and more distressed … he just needed to figure it out. He needed to find answers. He went over it all in his mind, telling himself "I'm not gay." But his mind would interject, "But what if you are? What if you really do like boys, and you're just lying to yourself? And … aren't you aroused down there?" He would check, and sometimes he was … but *what did that mean*? He couldn't stand the uncertainty. It was excruciating. He started avoiding looking at anyone who was male, and when that stopped working, he started avoiding going out at all. He started googling to see how you could tell if you were heterosexual or homosexual. He needed to know. If he just went over it all, one more time, in his head, maybe he would figure it out …

SHE FELT BETRAYED BY HER BODY

La'Keesha's stomach hurt—could it be cancer? She pushed away the thought. But her appetite wasn't so good these days—was that a sign? Could it be a tumor? Was it far along? She begged her mom to take her to the doctor again, to check. She must've missed something. Something was definitely wrong. She knew it. What if it was too late, and she couldn't be helped? Her heart began to race. "Oh no, here it comes, I don't want to feel this again"… and her arms and hands went numb. She couldn't think. The volcano of panic was building, and she would be out of control. What if her heart burst because it was pounding so loud? Was she going to die? As that thought began to spin faster and faster, her breath came shorter and shallower. The world receded and she was in full panic—she had to get out. Was there no end to this?

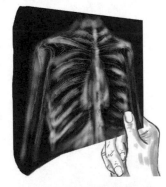

THEY ALL SPIRALED

OCD can attack in so many different ways. It can assault you with content about yourself, the world, the future. It can hurt you at the very core of your being. It can make you think you don't even have a core of your being.

So what do all these people have in common? It's not the content of their thoughts (or worries or body feelings). It's the patterns they're pulled into. It's the effort they are putting into not having these thoughts. They might do rituals that can be seen or rituals in their head. Those rituals are what tighten the spiral.

YOUR STORY

As you can see, there are so many different OCD spirals.

What does the stuff that's loud say to you? What images does it show you?

What does it tell you to do? What does it say will happen if you don't listen to it?

What does it say will happen if others find out?

How does it dictate your life?

What would you do if the stuff that's loud wasn't in control?

Chapter 3

STUFF THAT MAKES THE SPIRALS SPIRALLIER

The worst thing about OCD is probably the fact that you **feel trapped in a horrible cage that you yourself are responsible for building.**

Horrible things happen to many kinds of people every day. I don't want to undermine anyone else's struggle when I say that OCD is a different breed of hardship. It is not an outside force that is making your life difficult. It is your own brain that is doing this to you. Every time you complete a compulsion it may provide temporary relief, but at the same time it reinforces the cage you have trapped yourself in.

—Ethan

Think of the sneakiest thing you can think of.

Double it.

The stuff that's loud is sneakier.

Much sneakier.

It can pull you down a hole and then tell you that you're crazy for following it down the hole.

It can tell you that bad things will happen if you don't follow it. Really bad things.

Sometimes the stuff that's loud starts as a single thought. Other times there's an image. Or maybe your body tells you that something doesn't feel right. Or perhaps you have a really intense feeling of uncertainty or doubt. Then your mind tries to figure out what's wrong, so it explores the thought or image some more, and the awful feeling gets louder and more painful.

But if I have the same *thoughts* as a serial killer, how can I be *different* from a serial killer?

If I can't trust my *thoughts*, how do I know who I really am? If my thoughts are not me, do I even *exist*?

What if therapy makes me feel better, and then I feel okay about harming someone else?

I'M SO CONFUSED

And the thought or image or body sensation feels really awful so you try hard to get away from it, and you find some things to do that make you feel a bit better …

for a while …

but then the stuff that's loud sneaks back again …

and again …

and before you know it the stuff that's loud is spiraling and the things you do to try to make it stop make it spirallier.

As we saw in the last chapter, some people engage in mental gymnastics to help get rid of the thoughts or images. The stuff that's loud says that if you can just say this phrase to yourself in the right way or enough times or if you can just rehearse this enough times or just count these things enough times or …

Other people find that they need to check things and then check them again and then again …

Or clean things over and over …

Or not touch things that don't seem clean enough …

Or research and research and research …

but more information doesn't seem to lead to reassurance.

The more you fight the stuff that's loud, the more it fights back. The stuff that's loud spirals down and down and down, consuming more and more time and energy on the way down.

CONTROLLING THE WORLD AROUND YOU

There are other things you try that can make the world feel temporarily safer too (these are called safety behaviors). One common example is making sure you have excuses prepared in advance in case something goes wrong or so no one notices that you're always late (or early).

Maybe you've found others who are good at reassuring you that it's going to be okay or that the door is actually locked or whatever else the stuff that's loud is telling you isn't the case. Maybe the reassurance even helps.

For a little bit …

Perhaps you've become really good at researching and planning in advance so you feel like you know exactly what's going to happen in each situation and can plan what time to go and where to sit and what to say and what to wear and so on.

Maybe you have lucky objects you need to carry with you, or certain numbers that dictate what times or order you can do things.

What do you do to try quiet down the stuff that's loud?

Maybe you just find it easier to avoid things altogether.

Does your shower routine take too long? Maybe it's easier to just skip the shower.

Does eating certain foods take too much energy? Avoid them.

Are you exhausted when you need to go to particular places? Stay away.

How about those people or types of people who stress you out? Maybe it is just easier and safer and less exhausting to stay in your room.

Or in certain parts of your room.

Or in one exact spot.

Until that spot doesn't feel easy or safe. But by then moving no longer feels like an option either.

And you get stuck in your own head.

Trying to think your way to a safe space

Around and around and around

Looking for even one moment to rest your mind.

But it isn't there.

You can't even find that safe moment …

The stuff that's loud is so sneaky. It can create spirals within its spirals. And spirals for following the spirals. And spirals for not following the spirals.

Before you know it, your mind is busy beating you up for anything and everything. And your heart just feels heavy and sore. Your stomach aches. Your body is exhausted.

And then the shame sets in. And the self-doubt and self-blame.

It's humiliating; there is no way in the world you want anyone to find out how crazy you feel. But you also need others to reassure you. You need others around … and not around.

Your mind feels out of control.

Your emotions feel out of control.

The whole world feels out of your control.

Here's the thing that you need to know about the stuff that's loud:

IT'S LYING TO YOU!!!

It's not interested in the truth. It doesn't care about what is actually happening right now, nor what happened in the past, and has no desire to paint a realistic picture of the future. It wants one thing and one thing only, and that is your complete and undivided attention **at all times**.

It pulls all kinds of tricks:

It'll tell you to not talk to other people. It'll tell you to not go out. It'll tell you to not try to fight it. It'll tell you that no other thoughts or evidence can be trusted. It'll even tell you that you should be ashamed for listening to it. Or that someone will die or go to hell if you try to fight it.

It will say anything and everything it can to make sure that it has all your attention all the time. It will make you doubt things you've done. It will make you worry that you've done something really bad that you don't even remember doing. It might even make you doubt that you exist. It will make you check everything. It will make you feel WRONG or incomplete or full of dread …

It will wait until you're feeling pushed to your limit—stressed, alone, or vulnerable—and then say its worst things. It will find the things that matter the most to you and twist them beyond recognition.

It's like you're wearing headphones that can block out all other sounds so you can just listen to the stuff that's loud at maximum volume nonstop.

It doesn't only use words. It will paint pictures for you that are so convincing and compelling that they will feel completely true, deep deep in your gut. Or they won't feel true, but that "what if it is true ..." will niggle and squirm at the back of your neck, and just below your heart and at the side of your consciousness.

Or there will be no words. There will just be a sense of ... dread. Or wrongness ... or incompleteness ... not just rightness ... or perhaps your skin will feel ... crawly or dirty ... or things will feel ... dangerous, and you don't know why. But whatever it is will bother you ... and get louder ...

But here's another thing you need to know about the stuff that's loud:

Your mind is doing its job. You are not defective.

Your mind's number one job is to be on the lookout for danger, and to make sure that once you've spotted a danger you focus on removing or reducing the threat before you move on to other tasks. This is what minds are supposed to do.

Maybe your mind is doing its job too well and as a result it is incredibly difficult to do the things you want to be doing in your life.

Imagine Lisa is walking down the street thinking about what she wants to do this weekend or how much fun it was going to the beach last summer. But then suddenly she hears a loud ROAR!!!

Right away, Lisa stops thinking about the past or the future and focuses on the next few minutes. She loses sight of what matters to her and focuses on the danger. What made that sound? What dangerous things make that sound? Where is it coming from? Which direction should she move in? Where are her friends and family? Will they be okay where they are? Sure, the sound might just be a loud motorbike, but it also could be Godzilla, and Lisa will be safer if she assumes it could be a monster until she knows otherwise. Very quickly, the danger becomes all she can

think about. There's no mental space left to think about what else it might be or what else is happening this week. All she can think about is "How do I get away from Godzilla?" Assuming something new or unknown is dangerous until proven otherwise is an important survival skill.

It is true that the chances of a monster attack aren't that likely, but our minds are really good at imagining dangers and overestimating their likelihood. (And our news and social media sources know that—and stoke it.)

It's not just Lisa's mind that prepares for the worst-case scenario. Her body does too. Her heart rate increases, her muscles tense, her senses sharpen. Her body doesn't wait to find out if there really is a danger before preparing to flee. Instead it reacts in the way you would want it to if there actually was danger. This is a useful survival reaction, because it gives Lisa extra time to prepare for the danger.

It is this survival instinct that the stuff that's loud can exploit. All it needs to do is suggest a possible worst-case scenario, no matter how unlikely that might be, and your body will react as if it is actually happening or about to happen.

Then the stuff that's loud doubles down on sneakiness. It tells you what behavior you need to do to reduce the anxious feeling, and when you do what the stuff that's loud says, the anxious feelings do reduce—for a short while, which gives the stuff that's loud even more power. While you're doing what it tells you, there's no time left to do things that matter to you or connect with people you care about, so you feel even more anxious. And then it suggests a ritual to help reduce that anxious feeling.

Told you it was sneaky.

So you try to do something about it.

You ask for help or see a therapist or find a YouTube clip that tells you how to battle the stuff that's loud. It helps; you find something that works. Maybe you tell yourself it will be okay or that it's just OCD talking.

But then before you know it, the stuff that's loud has turned those things that help into rituals too. If you just tell yourself, "It's OCD" enough times, it will feel okay. Except it doesn't. So you need to say it again. Or seek new ideas. Or do more mindfulness exercises.

The stuff that's loud can make anything into a ritual.

Anything.

Including this book and the unspiraling ideas that we're going to talk about in the next few chapters.

Sorry.

So before you read the next chapter, please take a breath. And another one. Slow, deliberate, focused breaths. It's time to embrace the uncertainty and chaos that come with unspiraling.

Part Two

UNSPIRALING

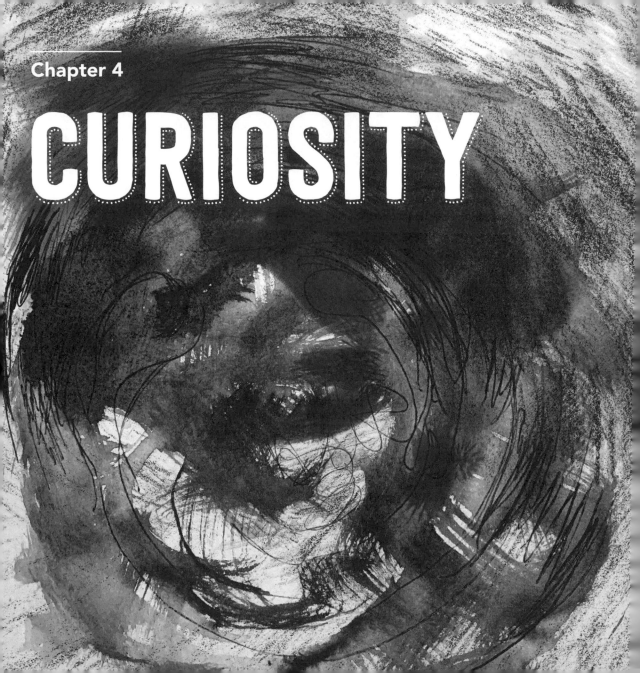

Chapter 4

CURIOSITY

The road is twisted.

It is steep and choked with thorns.

The view is worth it.

—Olivier Clarke

What if ...

Aren't you sick of your mind asking you that question?

How do you manage something that is so sneaky, such a blatant liar, and so demanding of all your attention?

How do you fight something that loves a good fight?

George Bernard Shaw said, "Never wrestle with a pig. You both get dirty, and the pig likes it." Your mind isn't a pig, but the stuff that's loud does enjoy a good wrestle. It dares you to provide evidence against what it's telling you so that it can discount your evidence and then laugh at you for even trying to engage.

The stuff that's loud wants to be the only thing blasting out of your headphones. It demands total domination of your perspective and your time.

So the first step in unspiraling is to notice that you're wearing headphones that are blasting out the stuff that's loud.

What if ... you choose to stop and notice?

Noticing is a deliberate choice.

When you watch a fantasy film, you can be so completely absorbed in the world of the film that it all feels completely true—the dragons and the dwarves, the magic powers and the time travel. As long as the internal logic of the film holds up, you don't start questioning how dragons can really breathe fire and fairies can fly.

Or you can choose to watch the film while maintaining your awareness that you're watching a film. You can marvel at how good the special effects are or focus on the costume your favorite actor is wearing. You could even step further back from the film and think about how this film compares to other films with the same actor or how it compares to the book it is based on. A good film tries to be so gripping that you don't step outside its world to notice these things, but being aware of all these layers can often actually increase your enjoyment of the film.

Music is the same. When you listen to music, you can be totally in the zone, letting the music carry you away with its emotion or groove. Or you might choose to shift your attention and notice what different instruments are doing in the song or read the lyrics and think about what the singer is trying to say.

What if … you could notice the stuff that's loud the way you can observe a film or music?

The stuff that's loud can be observed on different levels too. It does all it can to completely absorb us, so that it is all we can hear and all we can think about. It tries to be so gripping that you don't step outside its internal logic or pay attention to anything other than what it is telling you.

What if … there's much more to the story than your OCD is telling you?

What if … the first step toward finding out is … stepping back, and being curious?

Right now it's time to do some noticing. And to really notice things you're going to need lots of curiosity.

Imagine that this is the first time you've ever spent observing these things. See if you can notice things you've never noticed before.

Look around the room; what can you see? What shapes can you see? What is the light doing? What is happening in the shadows? How many shades of green can you see?

If you're in a familiar place, see if you can notice something you have never noticed before.

Notice different places where the air touches your body—is it warm or cold? What are you touching right now?

Notice that the stuff that's loud nearly always tries to pull you into the future …

…… or keeps you stuck in the past.

What if something bad happens?

What if I don't do my rituals correctly?

What if it's just like last time … and that was terrible?

What if it will always be like this?

The stuff that's loud doesn't like being in the present moment. Sure, it shows up here ALL THE TIME, but then it tries to whisk you away … so it's harder to notice what's going on RIGHT NOW.

Notice that the stuff that's loud is talking to you. Notice its sneakiness. Observe the ways it tries to be the only sound you can hear. Check out how truthy it sounds. It doesn't need evidence or logic; it just talks to you in its loud, confident voice and it becomes all you can hear.

And now it's time to play *what if?*…

Listen to what the stuff that's loud is telling you and spend the next thirty seconds doing what it tells you to do.

(tick tick … thirty seconds later …)

This time, listen to what the stuff that's loud is telling you and spend the next thirty seconds resisting what it tells you to do.

(tick tick … another thirty seconds pass …)

What happened? What was different between the thirty seconds when you did what the stuff that's loud tells you to do and the time spent resisting?

Now we invite you to try both of those things again. This time, spend a minute doing what it tells you and a minute resisting what it tells you. Go for it.

What felt different between the times you obeyed and the times you resisted? What happened in your body? Where did you feel discomfort? How long did it last?

The stuff that's loud tells you to expect the worst, that the feelings will never go away.

What happened when you noticed?

CURIOSITY IS YOUR FRIEND

The stuff that's loud demands certainty. It makes up stories and predictions about the future or reinvents the past and then demands that you believe all it says.

The stuff that's loud insists that things need to feel right. In your head or in your body. Maybe your body feels uneven, incomplete, or not just right.

The stuff that's loud also tells you what you can and can't do. Or what's too hard to do. Or what you can and can't handle.

What if

… there's a whole other story, just waiting for you to discover

> *… about how strong you are*

>> *… about what you can do*

>>> *… about how this all works?*

What if

… it's in the uncertainty where the magic happens? Only when we step into the unknown can we move our life in meaningful directions. Because when we stay in our certain places, our lives certainly stay still.

In order to unspiral and step into the world we want to be living in (rather than stay in the one the stuff that's loud tells us we need to stay in), we need to invite curiosity into our lives.

Let's begin by being curious about what the stuff that's loud is telling you. Notice the tone of voice it uses. Observe its sneaky and distorted logic. What happens when you don't do what the stuff that's loud tells you to do?

Does it get louder?

Does it stay louder?

Does it make threats?

Does it yell like a crazy dictator who is losing control?

The stuff that's loud is not going to play fair. It's going to try every dirty, sneaky trick it can think of to keep your complete attention at all times. It will lie. It will yell. It will throw big emotions at you. It might try to get you to feel overwhelmed, sad, scared, angry, frustrated, confused, ashamed, guilty, terrified … It will threaten havoc in your body too—heart racing, legs and arms tense, stomach doing backflips, tearfulness, shakiness …

Take a breath. Doesn't need to be a deep breath. Just the breath that your body can do right now. Take another breath. Remember that confident, strong, kind, wise voice you've selected to be alongside you as you take these bold, curious steps.

You've got this. Even though this is scary, you can do it. You're not alone.

Use your curiosity to notice all the tricks the stuff that's loud is throwing at you.

Use all your curiosity to notice what happens if you do what you want to do even when the stuff that's loud is telling you to do something different.

What if …

Okay, we're trying to make this sound simple, but we know it doesn't feel simple. We know that the first step is hard. You might feel like you're risking your health or your life or someone else's life or eternal damnation taking a curious step away from what the stuff that's loud is telling you.

We know we're asking a lot from you.

And please don't do it because we're asking you to.

Do it because you're curious about what will happen.

And if the first step feels too hard right now, then maybe there's a smaller first step you can take. It doesn't matter if you're taking a big step or a small step; all that matters is that you're curious about what will happen when you take the step.

Be curious about what happens when you let things feel uneven or just not right in your body. Even if just for a minute or two.

If it feels like the stuff that's loud is blasting at you from headphones, then be curious about what color or shape the headphones are. Notice whether you're able to hear any other noises in the room besides what the stuff that's loud is telling you.

Maybe the stuff that's loud is telling you things that you can't answer with curiosity. It might be telling you about things that will happen a long way in the future or even in the afterlife. Or it might be throwing stories about an imagined or forgotten past at you.

And even in the midst of that sneakiness, are you able to be curious about what's happening in the world around you right now? Notice the room you're in. **Be curious about the door and what's beyond it.**

Also notice what's happening in your body. What happens when things feel *uneven*? Or they just don't feel *just right*? Can you be curious about that sensation too? Even if only for a minute.

Curiosity might sound like hard work, but it can be fun. It is your friend on the path through OCD and other noisy thoughts.

Curiosity is like a muscle.

The more you use it, the easier it is to use when you really need it. So put on your mental gym clothes, your psychological yoga pants, because it's time for a curiosity workout.

Notice how many things the stuff that's loud can say to you in one minute if you give it a chance. Get some colored sticky notes and write down each thing it says (or paints—often the stuff that's loud hands us images instead of words). Don't forget to include the things it says to try to get you to not write the thoughts down.

What can you do with all those sticky notes? Make a pattern on the wall? Stick them all over your body? Put them on the floor and dance on them? Throw them in the air and watch how different notes float to the floor at different speeds?

Let's get even more confrontational. Listen to something the stuff that's loud says to you and write it on a piece of paper.

Then below it write: "The stuff that's loud is saying ..." (and again write down what it said to you).

Read each sentence back. Be curious about what each feels like. What happens when you notice that the stuff that's loud is talking to you?

And while you've got the stuff that's loud's words on your page, let's take your curiosity workout to the next level. What happens when you say those words really quietly? Then really loudly? Then in a really high voice? And in your lowest voice? Can you read the words backward?

If the stuff that's loud is handing you an image, can your curiosity have fun with that too? Can you sketch the image? Or imagine it black and white? Or zoom the picture out and see what else is hiding just beyond the edges of the original frame? How far out can you zoom?

If the stuff that's loud is a body feeling rather than a specific thought or image, then be curious about that. Examine the body sensation like you've never felt it before. Can you give it a name? Can you watch it move?

Now take one more step backward. Once you've noticed the things the stuff that's loud is saying to you, see if you're able to notice that you're noticing the things that the stuff that's loud is saying to you. Notice that you are separate from the stuff that's loud.

Notice the story that the stuff that's loud tells you will happen. Let's see what actually happens …

Maybe the stuff that's loud is telling you that writing or drawing down the things it says will make them more likely to occur or that others will think you're crazy or evil if they see what you're writing. We know that the stuff that's loud is a sneaky liar, and it's going to do all it can to block your curiosity.

It will probably even tell you that when you think these things you're making them more likely to occur. Yep, the stuff that's loud hands you a scary thought and then tells you that you're endangering yourself or someone else by thinking it.

Let's be curious about that threat too. 'Cause if you're able to make things true just by thinking them, then you are one powerful person. And with great power comes great responsibility.

So let's use your power. Right now, imagine that you're a superhero and can save the world. Imagine the sky turning green. In your mind, paint wings on your neighbor's dog.

How are you getting on making things true just by thinking them?

Or is the loud stuff lying to you when it tells you that you can make things true with your mind?

Or maybe you won't be able to see what happens because who knows what will happen in the future? But let's be curious about what's happening in your world right now, while you're listening to the stuff that's loud or not.

And speaking of sneakiness, start noticing the ways that the stuff that's loud is trying to steal the ideas we've already talked about and use them against you. Or even try to turn these ideas into more rituals.

If I just say "the stuff that's loud is telling me that …" enough times ,then it won't be able to hurt me anymore.

Or

What if someone sees what I've written down and decides I need to be locked up?

Or maybe

I know drawing the images of me hurting people probably won't hurt me, but what if it does?

We are not trying to be sneakier than the stuff that's loud. We don't have any magical formula that will make it shut up and leave you alone.

And at the same time, if you bring in some nondefensive curiosity and listen to your compassionate guide, maybe some more doors will open.

Are you willing to find out …

What if …?

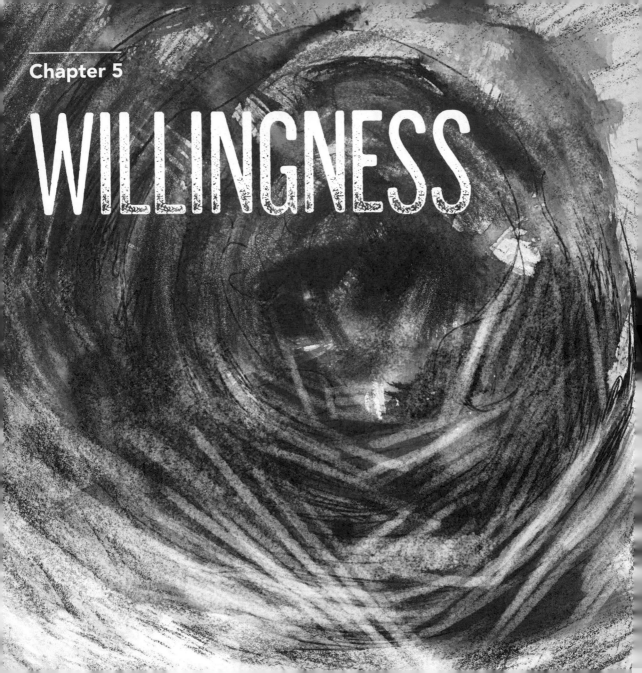

Chapter 5

WILLINGNESS

I remember the specific day that I told myself that I would overcome my OCD. I thought about how many people will never experience something so difficult in their lives. And that this may be the most difficult struggle I ever face as well.

After establishing that, I had another thought: If I can overcome this, if I can "lean in" and move toward helping myself, I could live the rest of my life knowing that I had conquered an adversary unlike any other. I could live with complete confidence that if I set my mind to it, I can do anything.

That day, I went out of the house for the first time in weeks. I said good-bye to my mom on my way out and looked her in the eyes when I did it. I then got on my bike and rode into the busiest part of town. Instead of covering my eyes, holding my breath, and completing countless other compulsions, I did the opposite. I looked for people who would give me anxiety. I looked to make myself uncomfortable. And while it may have been the hardest thing I have ever done, that day, I felt on top of the world. For every bit of discomfort I felt, I felt even more amazing knowing that I had proved to myself that I really can do anything. That day was the beginning of my getting better.

—Ethan

How do you do hard stuff? All those things you would like to do if only the stuff that's loud wasn't trying to stop you. Wanting it to be different isn't going to be enough. There's a reason it's called hard stuff. And we can do this.

Now that we've got our curiosity active, we can add **willingness**.

What does it mean to be willing? Does it mean to have WILLPOWER? Is that some kind of motivational product you can buy at a sports shop? Drink this and in an instant you'll be able to *WILL* yourself *to do whatever you want?*

We're sure others have made you feel like it should be that simple.

Does it mean completely wanting to do something? Waiting until that morning when you wake up and say, *"Hell, yeah! Bring on the ANXIETY AND DISGUST AND SENSE OF SHEER TERROR AND DREAD! LET'S FIND OUT IF I REALLY AM A SERIAL KILLER AFTER ALL—I'M TOTALLY PUMPED! WOOHOO!"*

Spoiler alert—you could wait until you're 150 and that day isn't going to come.

Also: sorry not sorry if we were a little bit triggering just there. It's just—we trust you. Your OCD/anxiety brain might think you can't handle stuff like that. We beg to differ. You've got this,

even when the stuff that's loud yells at you that you don't.

Here's the thing about unspiraling:

You'll never feel *ready*.

It will *never* be the right time.

You will never feel like, *I can 100 percent do this!*

It doesn't get easier/righter/better tomorrow, if you don't do it today.

Right this moment.

Ever go off a high dive? Like, the three-meter kind? If you have, then you know what we're talking about. If you haven't, imagine you are a little kid, scared of heights. You look up that waaaay tall ladder. Your little legs are burning, your knees knocking as you climb up. You feel the open air all around you, see the glint of the blue water far below. Then you step out onto the narrow board. "Don't look down," your mind says. "What if I fall," your mind says. "Freeze. You can't do this. It's too high."

So you stand there, trembling, or maybe you walk back to the top of the steps … and pause. And walk out to the end again … and freeze. And this goes on, over and over again. When you have OCD, your whole life becomes this little tiny shaky narrow space … where you could fall anytime … where you are trying. Back and forth, over and over again. Walking those same footsteps.

Trying really, *really* hard.

Back and forth. Back and forth. Waiting for it to get easier. For you to be ready. For it to be less scary.

And

    you

          are

               STUCK.

Sound familiar? Does it feel like your OCD has you trapped in a narrow little place where all you notice is how scared and uncomfortable you are, and you are *not moving*?

Does this feel like the opposite of willingness?

Hang on a sec—who is noticing that? You? Or your OCD?

For a second there, you had stepped back and were in that noticing place. WELL DONE!

Let's take this a step further—when you are unwilling to feel anxiety, do you feel safe?

Really slow down to notice this.

When is the last time you *really* felt safe? Or okay? Or like you finally did enough of the stuff OCD told you to do that you'd never ever have to do another ritual …

   … or check anything

      … or tap anything

        … or solve anything

          … or do mental rituals

            … ever again?

How long before you get triggered again, and the whole spiral gets spirallier … again?

When is the last time you *really* felt safe?

How long have you been stuck on that diving board?

Don't look down …

Notice that the loud stuff, sneaky as it is, tells you one story …

What if … there's a whole other story here for you to discover?

The key to that other story is willingness.

Willingness is saying yes to being scared.

Willingness is letting go of trying to control what you feel and think (because if you were able to control those things, you'd be doing it already).

Willingness is allowing yourself to be. It is seizing the moment, ready or not.

Willingness is letting yourself notice what you are feeling and thinking WHEN you feel and think it, and then being curious about the outcome. It can start small and grow as you lean into the *what if-ness* of the moment.

Willingness is a choice.

Willingness is not white-knuckling: it's not doing the thing you need to do but at the same time trying not to feel it, or think about it. It's not doing a hard thing, bracing yourself against it, and waiting until it's over.

Willingness is not tolerating being scared, pretending you're not scared or not wanting to be scared.

Willingness is not a thing that you either have or don't have; rather it's a thousand small steps.

Willingness may not be easy.

Sooner or later, you have to jump off the diving board whether you feel ready or not.

But what if I can't?

What if I splat?

What if it all goes wrong?

Minds are good at shutting down willingness. The stuff that's loud might tell you that willingness is a feeling and that you just haven't got it. Or that you can't be willing while you're anxious.

But what if that's just one more thing the stuff that's loud is telling you?

This is a good spot for you to get curious. Time for a high-intensity curiosity workout.

THE HIGH-INTENSITY CURIOSITY WORKOUT

Try a few of these:

ICE CUBE CHALLENGE:

Hold an ice cube in your hand. Let your hand feel the cold. Notice it. Notice how the experience changes.

WAITING IN LINE CHALLENGE:

Pay attention, on purpose, to how you feel waiting. Notice whether you're doing something to change your experience. If you are, quit it, and embrace the boredom/frustration/urgency you might feel. See what that's like.

EATING SOMETHING YOU DON'T LOVE CHALLENGE:

Brussels sprouts. Weird cheese. Licorice. A bug (no joke, Lisa did this). Listen to what your mind says to you, even as you read these words. Listen … and pop that thing in your mouth anyway. Notice what is going on in your mouth, your sense of taste, your feelings, your mind talking. Take your time.

WEARING TWO DIFFERENT SHOES CHALLENGE:

Ah, go on. Try it. Pay attention to what it's like. Notice whether other people even notice your two different shoes. Try out walking around in these mismatched shoes.

PEN-MARK ON YOUR FACE CHALLENGE:

Put a mark on your face big enough to be visible. We recommend not using a Sharpie or other permanent marker. Notice how your face feels. Pay attention to what your mind does with this. See what others do if they see it—and notice what your mind has to say about that.

GIVING UP THE LAST BITE CHALLENGE:

Of course you want the last bite of that pizza! No, you don't want to give it up! So do it anyway, and see what that's like.

GOING OUTSIDE IN THE RAIN CHALLENGE:

Rather than trying to stay dry, dashing between the raindrops, or making yourself smaller by hunching over, experiment with embracing the raindrops. Really getting wet. Notice their tender cold little pecks on your face. Catch them in your hands.

OTHER RANDOM IDEAS:

At the nail salon, close your eyes, point, and get whatever nail polish color you pointed at. Walk home on a different street that you're not used to. Try on clothes in a store you don't normally go to.

Notice everything!

Are you starting to get what we mean here? Think of something uncomfortable, and choose to do it. Say yes. Let your mind tell you aaaaaaaaaallll about what it will be like. We promise, the stuff that's loud will have a lot to say about this. **Do it anyway.**

Notice what that's like. Sloooooow down. Take off your coat. Stay awhile. Notice all the pieces of your experience—how your body feels, what your mind (or rather, your OCD) is saying, what feelings you are having. Get curious about what's in there, in this moment.

Did it feel how you expected it to?

Now time for another experiment. This time, instead of being curious and willing, try to *make yourself* do one of the challenges. Bully yourself into doing it. Notice how this feels.

Is it the same or different as when you chose *willingly*?

Notice that challenging yourself can either be a tug-of-war between you and your mind, or you could … choose.

You don't have control over thoughts and feelings. But you can always choose to be more or less willing.

You can *feel* willing, in your heart … and more importantly, you can *be* willing, by taking steps.

Make sure you stay awake—attuned to the here and now—to really see what happens.

Wonder. What happens next?

Are you ready to take the leap off the diving board?

(NO, says your mind.)

GREAT! We're not talking to your mind, we are talking to you! Your mind can come with you, though. It can stand alongside you on the board telling you not to do it, and you can still dive.

But where are we diving? *And why?*

Your mind might say, "To get away from my OCD." Or maybe, "To feel better."

Maybe.

But what if there's something more to this story? What if we can dive toward things we give a $#!% about, rather than just away from feelings we don't like?

Chapter 6

GIVING A $#!%

> *I would tell myself to not let OCD consume who I am.*
> *However long it takes to fight through it, that is okay.*
> *But make sure that when I come out, I'm still me.*
> *Make sure that I'm still kind, still lighthearted, still creative,*
> *and everything that I want to be.* —Ethan

These days there is so much pressure to feel happy and to be successful. Doing "okay" isn't enough. You might think that you need to be feeling awesome and doing awesome things and posting about those awesome things online and getting tons of likes and views. Because everyone else does, right? Does your mind tell you that story too? And do the whole social comparison thing? Ugh. Ours too.

You've already noticed that it isn't possible to feel happy and to be doing awesome all the time, because to do that you'd need to get rid of all anxious and sad feelings completely and forever, and no human being can do that.

You've already tried getting rid of those unwanted feelings. You've done everything the stuff that's loud tells you to try, hoping that eventually the feelings will go. Yet they're still here.

And there is only so much time in the day, and you've got only so much energy to use each day. And spending all your energy trying to get away from feelings and thoughts has been exhausting and not very effective.

But what other options are there?

What if you spent your time and energy moving toward the stuff you give a $#!% about—the people, things, and ideas that matter to you? Putting your energy into being how you want to be in this world and how you want the world to be?

Probably tons of people have asked you what you want to do with your life. They ask what job you want or what college you want to go to and so on.

Maybe you have some answers to these questions or maybe you don't. Or something in between.

And all those options are okay. All we're asking is that you look at the questions and the answers and the no-answers with curiosity.

If you know exactly where you want to go, we ask you to be curious about why that direction matters to you. What is it about that career or course of study or adventure that appeals to you? What relationships are important to you? What causes and issues do you want to be involved in? Will there be other ways you can move toward the same ideas even if the first path is blocked?

If you have no idea where you want to go with your life, can you be curious about what might be out there? If you could try stuff that you've never done before, what might you try? How about …

Asking someone to hang out? Someone you really like, but have been scared to talk to?

Signing up for a club or some volunteering?

Learning a musical instrument?

Trying a new sport?

Doing theater? Being in the spotlight, singing with your heart, bringing the audience to their feet?

Writing? Creating a world that you really enjoy spending time in, that others might dig too?

Skateboarding? At a really cool skate park full of other kids who look like they already know what they're doing?

Mountain climbing? Feeling the rough rock underneath your hands, as you pull yourself up into the blue sky?

Baking a cake for someone you love? Working on getting the icing the right color, noticing that wonderful smell coming from the oven?

Horseback riding? Galloping on a horse as fast as you can?

Notice any ideas that feel uplifting … sort of like you are going up in a hot air balloon? Even though your worries are yelling at you, giving reasons why these things can't be options, are there things that feel exciting or fun or interesting as you think about them? What might you discover about yourself if you tried new stuff? Sometimes when you aren't sure what you care about, your mind will try, in its risk-averse way, to help you think your way to an answer. BUT it's likely you'll discover more about what's important to you by doing stuff—rather than just thinking about it.

Or maybe you're somewhere in between—you've thought of a direction that matters to you, but your mind says something like "Never gonna happen," and you get stuck in that thought. Or the stuff that's loud has told you not to listen to those parts of you that dream of moving forward.

All options are okay. It's totally fine to know or to not know or to half know. Wherever you are, please be curious about the stuff that matters to you. The stuff you give a $#!% about.

Are you interested in discovering what matters to you? Try this:

Make a bucket list. What's that, you say? That is all the stuff—and we mean really all the stuff—possible or impossible—that you might have dreamed about doing during your lifetime. Or thought about doing. Or wanted to do. Or thought was too crazy or improbable to do. If there are people you want to do these things with, write that down too, for each item on your list. Write down as many things as you can think of. Your mind will probably say, "Never gonna happen." Write them all down anyway …

Go on, write it now …

Keep writing, see how many ideas you can get on your page. See if you can write twenty, even if some feel far-fetched.

When you have a good bunch of these—and the more the better—take a good look at them, and start crossing out the ones that are the least important. Keep only the TOP five.

Is there something that ties all these together? Something underneath them, that is what each of these things is *about*? Does thinking about that thing make you feel … alive? Hopeful? Scared? Inspired? If so, notice that. Your heart is trying to tell you something about what makes you tick; about what makes you, well, you. It's the stuff that you give a $#!% about.

At this point, you might notice your OCD chiming in with something like …

But you have to deal with ME first. ME ME ME.

And you might begin to spiral down again …

Just like always. It's almost like a rule your mind tells you: FIRST get rid of the OCD, and THEN you get to have your life.

But … what if it's time to change the rules?

Change rules? How?

Confused? You might be feeling a little lost …

GETTING LOST

Sometimes the best way to get to know a place is to get lost in it. To step out of the familiar streets of your internal map.

In order to do that, you'll need to notice all your efforts to do away with your stuff that's loud for a bit, and then choose to look up, look for new unexplored directions.

Let's take a few minutes to think about rules … like the one about how you have to get rid of your loud stuff in order to have a good life.

And as well as your own self-imposed (or OCD-imposed) rules, parents, school, government all have rules for you.

Mostly these rules are in place to reduce the risks to you and others. For example, wear your seat belt! Use the crosswalk! Don't smoke! Sometimes this is great! And helpful! Other times, you might feel constrained. You might feel like you're being treated like a little kid, even when you're supposed to be learning how to adult.

Parents and the systems around you know best. Until they don't. You only need to watch the news for a few minutes to know that adults haven't figured out the answers. Adolescence is about discovering—about finding your life. Around the world, teenagers are questioning the rules that are hurting people or the planet we live on. We see young people asking the hard questions and making important decisions and calling out the adults around them. Making the world better by challenging beliefs and actions about the environment and fighting prejudice and broadening the range of acceptable life options.

Consider Greta Thunberg, for example. She's a young person from Sweden with her own loud stuff, including OCD. When she was a little girl, she became very concerned about climate change. She couldn't understand why none of the adults in her life were doing anything about it. She realized that for herself, and others her age, the world would become a very different, much hotter, much less livable place than it is right now.

When she was sixteen years old, Greta decided to do something about it. She broke the rules: She started a school strike on Fridays. By herself. She made signs and sat outside the government buildings in Sweden, week after week.

One by one, others joined her—young people from all over the world. She spoke at the United Nations, and the World Economic Forum. She gave a TED talk. She was nominated for the Nobel Peace Prize. And now, people listen to her. She said, "Once we start to act, hope is everywhere. So instead of looking for hope, look for action. Then and only then, hope will come today."

Greta stepped off the map of what she was supposed to do and changed the rules. Instead of thinking about it, she acted. And when she did, she created hope.

How about the confining map that OCD tries to keep you on? This narrow map that developed to keep you and others safe, and inside your comfort zone? (Even though the zone probably stopped feeling comfortable a long time ago, and the rules feel more like a prison.)

If you are stuck on an OCD map, then you have rules that are holding you back. The stuff that's loud wants to be safe too. So it gives you lots and lots of rules, usually starting with "Don't …" or "Be careful …" or "You can't …"

If you are in an OCD story, how are you going to learn if you can't try new things sometimes? How are you going to know how something works until you take it apart and put it back together again?

It's time to change the rules and expand your map. It's time to be curious, and act. Being an adolescent is about exploring the world and developing your own rules along the way. When you step out of your own OCD story and start working on stuff that you care about, you can make new rules that will help you get closer to what matters to you. As you learn more and see more, the rules can keep evolving to match where you are, what you want to be doing, and the person you want to become. You can become an explorer in the adventure of your own life.

So what makes a good explorer?

Before the sixth century BCE, people thought the earth was flat. And between the sixth century and the fifteen hundreds there was a whole truckload of uncertainty. Maybe the earth was flat. Maybe not. Nobody really knew.

So what would it take for somebody to say, Hey! What a cool idea to face sudden death by sailing off the edge of a flat earth, where on the way there are probably dragons and man-eating sea monsters of all kinds! And also, I don't know how to swim! GREAT! Let's do it!

Insanity? Maybe.

Death-defying bravery? Perhaps.

Curiosity? For sure.

What about a dream? A really big dream, one that was bigger than the fear explorers must've felt, and bigger than the obstacles in their way?

In 1977, the Voyager 1 and 2 spacecrafts were launched into space. Their mission was to explore Jupiter and Saturn. On Voyager 1 was the Golden Record, which included a gold-plated disk that held recordings of sounds and images selected to portray life on Earth.

The scientists involved depended on two really different kinds of what-ifs. The first kind was all about problem solving, because about a million things could go wrong and make the mission fail. And the team needed to anticipate and solve as many possible problems as they could in order for the mission to go forward.

If they had stopped there, there probably wouldn't have been a mission. After all, it seemed so insurmountable, so expensive, so improbable. The longest of long shots.

But they didn't stop there, because they also had a different kind of what-if, one that was much bigger than all their doubt and uncertainty.

What if we could learn something about our place in the universe? What if we could see something we've never seen before, from a totally different perspective than we thought possible? What if that would help us understand humankind, our planets, our place in the galaxy? What if we could send a message out to other possible worlds, to see if we are not all alone here?

So the scientists did all the problem solving they could, and then they took a giant leap, and launched the spacecrafts.

What if …?

The Voyager mission was expected to last approximately five years.

Today, this very minute, Voyager is still going. On August 25, 2012, Voyager 1 crossed into interstellar space, followed by Voyager 2 on November 2, 2018. These spacecrafts are the farthest human-made objects from our planet, still sending back data from the stars. This is well beyond what anyone in their wildest dreams ever thought possible.

What makes a good explorer?

Not the absence of fear.

Not feeling ready.

Not knowing for certain everything would be okay.

Instead …

    … curiosity …

        … willingness to discover, even when there might be dragons …

… and a really big dream that sets your heart on fire

        … that inspires you to go big,
            or go home

        … and makes being afraid worth it.

How do you touch with your heart what's important to you? How do you discover your inner adventurer? What could be big enough, inspiring enough for you to risk shame, isolation, dragons, zooming into interstellar space for?

Is it scary to even ask these questions? *What if it all goes wrong?*

So let's ask some big questions.

Imagine your world without OCD or the stuff that's loud. Gone. Yes, we know your mind is saying this exercise is pointless and impossible. It may even hurt to imagine something different from your "now," or make you sad, or feel lost because a different life feels so far away. Let that feeling come along for the ride. Imagine anyway.

Imagine you're given a time machine. It's really cool—it can take you ten years into the future. So you jump into the machine, push the buttons and KAZAAM you're in the future. And surprisingly, stuff is actually great. The first thing you notice is that the people around you are the people you most want around.

(Pause here, take in a breath, and give this question some loving consideration.)

Who is there with you?

Next you notice that you are doing stuff that is interesting to you and inspires you. You love being in this future. It's not necessarily that you have *stuff*. It's that you are engaged in your life, doing things that matter to you.

Spend a few minutes imagining what this life is like.

What are you doing? Why do these things inspire you?

Imagine you've built yourself a life that you love—really LOVE. In it are people who love you, and things you do that make you feel inspired. Getting up in the morning is *joyful*. Yes, really. Imagine.

Imagine YOU have built yourself this life. It was hard work. There were a ton of times you were sure you'd hit your wall, that you couldn't do it. There were lots of times things didn't follow your initial plan, and you had to regroup and start again. And yet you did. All of your effort … every hard day … each step … led to this.

If you could be anywhere, where would you be ten years from now? Close your eyes and picture it. Take some time. What do you look like, in this life? This one, that you built?

Imagine that this Future You could travel back in time to visit you now. What would Future You—from this place where you have arrived, in this life you love—tell you now? What advice would they give you?

Take a few moments to listen. Listen close.

When your OCD gets in the way, you will have a choice to make:

Forward or………….. stuck?

What if ...

... each time you leaned into your OCD you took a step closer to a life you could love? Maybe one you lost—that your spiraling took away from you—or maybe one you get to build the way you wish?

Go out and explore your world. And beyond...

Chapter 7

FLEXIBILITY

The first step is not the hardest. I think it is certainly hard to take that first step toward facing your OCD and your fears, but it is not the hardest or the most important. The hardest step is the second step, and the third step, the fourth, and all the steps that come after that.

Just because you fought back once does not mean you are in the clear. To get better takes the perseverance, effort, and vigilance to be constantly ahead of your illness and to keep working until you are satisfied. —Ethan

Rules can keep us stuck. All rules get us stuck sooner or later. So in order to unspiral, you'll need flexibility. To find ways to follow rules that are helping you get closer to the people, things, and ideas that matter to you, and change your rules when they're getting in the way of you being the kind of person you're working toward being everywhere you want to go.

THE STEPS

The first step: Make a promise to yourself about something that really matters. An example might be the kind of person I want to be isn't the kind of person who is held back by my OCD, so I'm going to choose not to let myself do a ritual for the next ten minutes, no matter what. Out of the question! Keep this promise in your head for the next two steps!

The second step: Start small. If you're not willing to resist doing rituals for ten minutes, then do five minutes. Or two minutes. Or thirty seconds. Just whatever you do, choose. Notice when it's harder and when it's easier. Use what you notice to make a menu of scary, hard, loud stuff, and work out what rituals (or flat-out avoidance tactics) you typically do to make yourself feel better. Do the hard stuff in whatever order you like. Don't do the rituals.

The third step: Repeat the second step. Keep it up. Practice everywhere, everywhen, everyhow, everymood, with everyone. Don't stop.

These three steps are called exposure and response prevention, or ERP. It's how you teach your OCD mind that no matter how loud it gets, you're not going to do what it says.

It's also how you teach yourself that if you let OCD talk to you, right up in your face and super loud, it doesn't have power over you.

Now for the how.

Be curious. Wonder what will happen if you do what the loud stuff doesn't want you to do. Impossible? Let's find out!

Pay attention. Notice everything. Slow down. Open up.

Turn toward the loud stuff. Make the scary, gross, uncomfortable, uncertain places cool spaces to hang out in. Lean in—and *don't* do the thing you normally do (or anything else, for that matter) to make yourself feel better. Notice the stuff that scares you, makes you uncomfortable, makes you disgusted or horrified or terrified or uncertain. Notice when those feelings show up.

Watch for OCD thoughts. Listen to what your OCD says will happen. Very likely, your OCD will have a lot to say about you not doing what it wants. It will get LOUD, right up in your face. Don't give in!

Be willing. Let thoughts and feelings wash over you. No need to defend yourself from them. Get to know them. Pay attention on purpose to all the different shades and nuances of each feeling. Where does it show up? Notice that there is room inside you for this feeling. Notice that there is space for the thought that there is no space for this thought. Notice all the feelings that show up

in your body with the thoughts—feel their edges. Notice where they begin and end. Step back from your thoughts and observe them. Be willing to let OCD say whatever the heck it wants.

One way to work on your willingness is to rightsize your exposures. You can come up with what we call a hierarchy, or a list of stuff to do that starts small and gets really big and scary. And if you like, you don't have to go from small to large—you can jump around too! Make a menu instead of a *hierarchy*. As you launch yourself toward the stuff that really matters, the stuff that's loud might get in your way. Take those opportunities to avoid doing rituals. Improvise. Do over-the-top scary stuff!

An example might help. Let's say your stuff that's loud tells you that you need to check stuff, or else something terrible will happen. Think of Adam, in the **Stuff That Spirals** chapter—he needed to check and google and ask for lots of reassurance that a meteor wasn't going to destroy the earth.

Adam might…

Start with drawing a picture of a meteor.

And then lots of pictures of meteors.

Little ones, then bigger, scarier ones.

And then carry them around in his pockets, or put them on his bedroom wall, right over his bed.

All the while, he might *resist* asking for reassurance. And if he asks his mom, for example, he might have her say, *That sounds like your OCD talking. No need to answer that question.*

And THEN he might write scripts about what would happen if (WHEN) a meteor hits the planet. And those scripts or stories might get more and more detailed over time.

And THEN he might tell his mom to show him stuff from the Internet about meteors hitting the earth.

MAYBE he would visit a museum where there are actual meteors!

Maybe he'd watch a movie (there are several) where giant meteors are going to hit the earth.

MAYBE when he goes to leave for school he has his family say, *Hope a meteor hits you on your way to school!*

You get the idea. If you have this kind of stuff that's loud, you are probably pretty triggered. GOOD. That means we are headed in the right direction! The more triggering the ERP is, and the more willing you are to experience it, the better the learning will be!

As you work through your ERP hierarchy or menu, don't accidentally (or on purpose) do rituals. If it feels scary and bad, you're doing it right. If you do something to make yourself feel better or to keep control, or reduce uncertainty, it's probably a ritual. If you try to distract, or rush through, or just get it over with, you're probably white-knuckling.

Give a $#!%. We know it's tough to choose to do ERPs, so it can be super helpful to work them into your life, into activities that are consistent with the stuff you give a $#!% about. For example, start by imagining yourself doing a tough ERP so that you can build yourself a life that you love. Picture it. Notice what OCD says when you do this. Let it be as loud as it wants!

Be flexible. Take it on the road. If you practice in the same place, in the same mood, with the same people all the time, you'll probably notice that your OCD is louder in places you haven't practiced. If you are feeling more vulnerable—like if you are tired, or feeling anxious about something else, or grouchy—you might notice OCD raising its volume. That's okay. It simply means that these are new places and contexts where you should practice ERP. Try ERP in all sorts of places.

Mix things up. Jump around when you do your exposures. You could do them easiest to hardest, or you could do them randomly—either way

is okay. Capitalize on unexpected exposures. Improvise exposures. If you feel triggered by something unexpected, practice thinking that this might be a great opportunity for exposure. For example, let's say that Adam is walking outside on the beach at night with his girlfriend and sees some shooting stars. Immediately, the stuff that's loud is back, looking for certainty and reassurance. Instead of hiding his fear, or asking his girlfriend for reassurance, Adam might take a deep breath and say, *Did you see those shooting stars? What if they were huge meteorites heading toward the earth? Sometimes I get these scary thoughts … and they are loud. Let's see if we see any more shooting stars, and stay out here a bit longer, looking at the sky. It's beautiful, isn't it …* even if his OCD says it's ALSO pretty scary.

Change your perspective. Once upon a time, there was just you and OCD. Think about your relationship with it. Did you (or do you) have a hard time telling where OCD ends and you begin? Did you (or do you) think you're OCD?

What if you thought of OCD as another person, or a character in a book? How would you describe it? Would it be bossy? Crazy? Kind? Paranoid? Gentle? What would it look like? If you could imagine the sound of its voice, what would it sound like? Gruff? High-pitched and whistly?

What if you imagined that your OCD was like a little child, hiding behind a chair in the corner, waiting for you to take it by its hand and show it how to be courageous? How would your relationship to OCD change if you imagined it like that?

Screw it all up, and try again. This is maybe the most important step. You will mess up, or give in, at some point. Then your mind will tell you you've failed, and you can't do it, and there's no point. Of course. We told you that OCD is ninja-level sneaky.

As you go through your ERP practice, you might notice that when you make headway in one area, the stuff that's loud might pop up again, in another place. For example, if you did meteor-hitting-the-earth ERPs, and those thoughts now come and go without you getting spiraled up in them, NOW you might have intrusive images of harming someone physically or sexually. And you might think, "Crap. My stuff that's loud is LOUDER now, and this ERP stuff doesn't work." Or "Maybe there IS something wrong with me, and I just can't do it." THAT is a good example of the stuff that's loud tricking you again. Remember, *what the thoughts are about doesn't matter*. It's about the pattern—scary thought or feeling, urge to do a compulsion or ritual, and then the spiraling begins again ... UNLESS you notice the new loud stuff for what it is—sneaky old OCD, trying to spin you in again.

Keep going. Keep going. Keep going.

Cool ERP Ideas

Work *just outside your comfort zone*.
When you practice ERP, it's best if you are
working in a zone where you are willing to be
uncomfortable. If you stay inside your comfort
zone, you'll never stretch it and make it bigger!
In fact, OCD often steals ground and can make
your comfort zone smaller … and smaller …
and smaller … maybe until you can't move or
think at all.

To work outside your comfort zone is to make it
bigger—to give yourself more room to move and
live and love and breathe. It can make you feel
so vulnerable to be outside your zone. Learn to
hang out there. Spend some time. See the sights.
Then step beyond *that* zone. Onward.

Mix it up. There are a million and one ways
to do ERPs. It can be helpful to talk to an ERP
therapist to help you come up with ideas that are
right for your OCD. Fine-tuning your ERPs can be
super important. Here are some examples:

 If you miss your friends, call them,
text them, go visit them. If OCD shows
up, don't just white-knuckle it—really be
with your friends. Give them your whole attention.
Appreciate what it's like being with them, even with
OCD there too.

 If your OCD tells you that you need to
move a certain "just-right" way, choose
to go to a place that matters to you—
and move in a "just-wrong" way.

 If your OCD makes you scared of
particular thoughts, like harm thoughts,
then make signs with those thoughts
and put them up in your room. Count each time
you look at them and *don't* tell yourself it will be
okay. This is even more powerful if you are also
worried about what people would think if they
knew you had these thoughts.

If scary OCD thoughts pop into your
head, make a study pack of index cards
with a scary thought written on each
one. Keep them with you. You can start with just
one if you need. Pull the cards out from time to
time, in different settings, during the day, and

look at them. When you've built up a few, add random words, like "banana" mixed in there, so you never know which one you'll get. If you are doing ERP with harm thoughts, add in the names of people you're scared you might harm to the deck.

 If your OCD makes you worry about there being poison or contamination in your food, go to the coffee shop, and when they ask you what you want, say, "I don't know. What's good?" and get that.

 If OCD says your stuff needs to be organized just so, mess it up! Leave it there.

 If your OCD makes you want reassurance from other people, don't ask. Instead, tell on yourself to those who are helping you with your OCD. For example, say, "I'm pretty sure I just committed a mortal sin; don't tell me I didn't."

 On the other hand if your OCD tells you that you need to confess, don't say a word. Zip it. Notice the discomfort.

 If you do rituals in your head—like saying certain things in a certain way, or even giving *yourself* reassurance— resist that and lean into the feeling of discomfort or uncertainty.

 Do ERP bingo. Mix it up. Do improvised ERPs. Capitalize on when you are surprised by an unexpected trigger. Life is unpredictable!

Go after ERP! You might start out by thinking "Okay, I won't let my OCD make me do this ritual," but then try moving toward really *pushing* your OCD, like "I wonder what would happen if I did THIS?" If you notice your OCD getting louder about something, think "THIS would be a GREAT ERP! I'm gonna do it!"

TROUBLESHOOTING

Make sure to work in the places and on the tasks where you are willing to be in contact with uncomfortable, triggering thoughts. Remember, to be willing doesn't mean wanting to do an ERP, or *liking* it, or *being ready* to do it. It just means that you willingly choose to put yourself in situations where you are triggered and anxious and uncomfortable AND still resist doing rituals.

Don't *make yourself* do ERPs. OCD does enough of making you do stuff anyway. Your power lies in choosing, and noticing that you are choosing to do hard stuff, no matter how loud OCD is, because you've made a promise to yourself that really matters.

It can be hard to tell what's a ritual and what's not. And sometimes, sneaky OCD can co-opt good stuff you are doing and make that into a ritual. When your OCD is loud, anything you do that makes you feel better/less anxious/less uncomfortable/more certain or relieved is probably a ritual.

If you get stuck, don't give up. Know that almost everyone gets off track—it's not a straight path. Instead, it's really treacherous and goes over rocks and through swamps and … and … You are not alone. Ask for help. Talk to an ERP therapist.

Keep in mind that your OCD will sometimes be loud and sometimes be quiet, even if you keep doing ERPs. That's okay. It will probably get quiet after lots of ERP practice. The trick is, if and when it gets loud again, remember, *you KNOW what to do*. Be curious, be willing, be flexible.

Remember the three steps … no matter how loud it gets, you're not going to do what it says.

Be kind to yourself when you are working hard, and especially when you fall down. Celebrate your successes, no matter how small. They are all steps in the direction of the life you will build for yourself.

Tune in to that kind, strong, and wise voice. It is with you on this difficult path.

Once you start seeing that there are little things you can do, and you start making a little bit of progress, it's amazing how satisfying it is, and how much you can start going after it. I started wanting to go after it. It stopped being "I can't let myself do this," and being more like "I want to challenge myself and see what I can do." And once I caught that wind, I sort of sailed on from there.

—Ethan

YOUR PARENTS, AND WHAT TO DO WITH THEM

Well done for making it to Chapter 8. Have we sparked your curiosity? Have you identified things you're willing to try and try them flexibly? Have you identified the things you give a $#!% about? If you've already been experimenting with the ideas we've shared so far, take a pause and step back for a moment. Breathe. Notice.

Consider what the cost of struggling with your OCD has been in your life. What might it be like for you to unspiral? What would it be like to be curious, rather than simply doing what the stuff that's loud says? To be willing to feel uncomfortable stuff? To live flexibly, outside of OCD rules?

What if simply asking these questions is a powerful thing that could shift you into a different sort of life—one you love? Into *freedom*?

You've probably felt trapped for a long time. And just as the stuff that's loud has kept you in a cage, very likely it's trapped those around you too.

Especially your family and friends. Because the stuff that's loud can have impacts on other people as well. It can be really hard for others around you to see you suffering, so they might try to make you feel better by reassuring you, or helping you with your rituals, or letting you just stay in your room/on the couch/in bed because you feel like it's too hard to do anything else. That's called *accommodation*, and it can feed your OCD.

Other stuff can happen too. You might have found really effective ways to get people to help you in the short term—maybe yelling or screaming, or worse. Maybe stuff you're not proud of. We all get it wrong sometimes, even when we're trying to do our best. And when we get it wrong, we apologize and try to act differently next time.

OCD can drag in your family. When it's really loud, your family life becomes about the care and feeding of the stuff that's loud. Normal family life slips away. Parents might blame themselves or blame you for your OCD. Siblings might become resentful or embarrassed. Friends might give up asking you to do things or stop expecting you to show up. Of course, all these things make it harder to unspiral. It's likely you also feel crappy about some of the ways the stuff that's loud has led you to treat others.

All these strong feelings make the OCD very hard for the family to talk about. **OCD thrives in secrecy.** It makes itself the center of everything by becoming the thing that nobody is talking about. It becomes the biggest secret at the heart of your universe.

Be curious about all the important conversations you're *not* having with your parents and friends and siblings. What are you not saying to them? What does your OCD not allow them to say to you?

What percentage of the time are you hanging out, doing regular family activities … and what percentage of the time is occupied by OCD and everyone keeping quiet to accommodate it?

If you are trying out the ideas in this book, you are working so hard to grow your curiosity, your willingness, and your flexibility. You've thought about what you give a $#!% about and are taking steps toward those things. Now we really want to **bring the stuff that's loud into the light to reduce its power even more.**

In this chapter we're going to give suggestions for how you can talk to your parents about what you're going through and how they can help you—and your family—unspiral. You might want to try some of these words, or you might have your own words. Either way, let's get talking.

There's me and there's my OCD.

Sometimes it's hard to keep these separate, but I am learning where I begin and my OCD ends.

THINGS YOU MIGHT WANT TO SAY ABOUT OCD

OCD is when I get caught in a spiral.

Thoughts, images, or feelings come up that feel loud, true, and terrifying, and I often feel wrong or crazy for even thinking them.

So I try really hard to keep away from this stuff that's loud.

— I do some rituals in my head.
— I do some rituals that can be seen.
— I avoid some places or activities.
— Sometimes I even get you to help me with my rituals or avoidance.

I know you've seen me do some of these things. And there are still a lot of things you haven't seen me do.

Sometimes it feels like I have no control over them.

Sometimes it feels like I can't help yelling.

Sometimes I feel desperate, sometimes I'd rather just … stop … and not be … just so I don't have to listen to OCD anymore.

And sometimes it's easier to do nothing at all, because if I do *anything* that means I will have to do a ton of rituals.

Sometimes it feels impossible.

But I'm not going crazy. OCD is an anxiety disorder, and it is more common than we know because it is so hard for people to talk about and can take people so many years to ask for help.

THINGS YOU MIGHT WANT TO SAY ABOUT <u>YOU</u>

I'm not doing my rituals to be difficult or to get attention. I do my rituals because they feel like a "have to" that's really, really hard to resist. It can even feel like people's lives depend on me doing my rituals.

I've been dealing with this for a long time, longer than you've even noticed. Sometimes I've managed doing things without you discovering how hard and how terrifying it was for me to do. Other times I responded by being upset or angry.

And I've been trying really hard to reduce the power that the OCD has over me. This book has given me some ideas to try too. I'm trying to be curious, willing, and flexible.

I (like every other human on the planet) have good days and bad days. Every day, I push myself and do what I'm able to do, but just because I can manage something one day doesn't mean I've got it mastered for life. We all take steps forward and backward.

THINGS YOU MIGHT WANT TO SAY TO YOUR PARENTS ABOUT HOW THEY CAN HELP

OCD is super loud. And I often don't know how to handle it. I'm trying. I'm going to screw it up, so please be patient with me. I'm learning.

This is the hardest thing I've ever done. And much as I want to be independent, I need your help. I'm scared to say that, because a big part of me just wants you to tell me it will be okay. But I need you to not do that.

It won't be easy, and sometimes I won't react in ways that are helpful. I'm sorry.

There may be stuff that pops into my mind that I'm afraid to tell you. I'll work on learning to talk about the things that scare me, but it may take some time.

Just know, even when OCD is loud, and I seem totally different from that sweet little kid I once was, I'm still in here. I'm stuck, and I'm working my way out.

When I was small, I know you always wanted to protect me and keep me safe. Now is the time to help me learn to be brave, *even when I'm asking for you to reassure me*. Even though I know it might be hard for you to watch me being anxious, I want you to know it's okay. We can do this.

It's going to feel weird and wrong letting me be anxious. Your mind might be telling you that good parents don't let their children feel scared or sad or stuck. I promise you that's just what I need. I can handle it. I don't need you to solve it for me, but I do need you there, no matter what, especially when I'm at my most stuck.

Sometimes I'll need your help resisting my rituals, or help noticing when I'm avoiding something because of the OCD. I need you to encourage me to go out and explore and discover my own strengths. I need you to believe they are there, even when I can't see them. Especially when my OCD says I'm weak.

I'll fall down a lot and you'll feel frustrated because some days will be harder than others. It won't be a straight path. Please know I'm trying.

Celebrate the small wins with me. Because the small wins all add up to something bigger. Something that matters.

It's okay to ask me more about what I'm struggling with, and you can borrow this book from me if you want to learn more about OCD.

As a family, we need to look out for times when someone is helping me do the rituals, either willingly or unwittingly. I know you do this because you think it would help. Our whole family needs to understand that **if the family *accommodates* OCD, we are all allowing it to rent space in our home, in your family.** This isn't anyone's fault any more than having OCD is my fault—it's just that this is how OCD changes the way families work. It spirals others in too.

In order for our family to unspiral from OCD, we'll all need to resist my OCD rituals. It will be hard for me and hard for you. Let's work together to notice ways in which we're allowing the OCD to be sneaky or secretive. Let's work together to bring it into the light where it has less power.

If I ask for reassurance, maybe family members can ask, "Is that you or your OCD talking right now?"

Instead of saying "It's all going to be okay," maybe family could say, "I'm not sure. Maybe it is, maybe it isn't. Let's just see what happens."

If I'm in a new situation where I haven't practiced much ERP and the OCD becomes really loud, then family can remind me that this is a great learning opportunity. The louder it is, the better the learning.

Mostly I just need to know that you're in my corner, no matter what.

HOW AND WHEN TO TALK TO PARENTS

Okay, so that's a big list of things you might want to let them know. But it doesn't all need to be in one conversation or at one time. In this book we've broken down the steps of unspiraling from OCD by being **curious, willing,** and **flexible.** Ask your parents to talk with you about what you've read so far in this book. Or lend the book to them!

It's important for us to mention that *this book isn't therapy*. It's a *guide* that you and your parents can use to start unspiraling and to take some steps in your chosen directions. Hopefully you're able to do this work with a therapist who is skilled in ERP, and who has experience working with OCD.

You may be reading this going, "I'm just not ready to say all this." That's okay. But can you say some of it? Can you start the conversation?

It can be helpful to plan out what you want to say when you have a clear head. Don't wait till you are in the middle of an OCD crisis and then try to explain what's going on.

When do you have your best discussions with your parents? Late at night? In the car? On the weekend? Trying to explain things to them while everyone is at their most stressed probably isn't going to be the most effective time to talk. Try to pick a time when they are calm, and not rushing from one thing to the next, or working on getting you to do something.

Do you want to talk to one parent first or talk to them together (assuming you have two parents that you're talking to)? Is there another adult you want to talk to first and have them help you talk to your parents? Sometimes it helps to talk things out first … even to yourself, in the mirror, before launching into it with your parents.

Chapter 9

BUILDING AN ARMY

OCD likes to divide and conquer. It's important to remember that you are not alone.

Social isolation is bad for your health.

We can't stress this enough. We get that you need your alone time to recharge. But human beings were designed to be social creatures. We learned to work in groups to catch food, build homes, raise families, and just generally support each other.

OCD loves to keep you all to itself. It demands so much of your attention that being with others can feel impossible. It will use so many dirty tricks in order to keep you isolated. It will tell you that no one else will understand what you're dealing with. It might make you feel ashamed of all you're thinking and doing. It tells you that there's no time to see people because you've got important things to do or that you'll have to do too many rituals if you see others.

As you've probably noticed throughout the book, if the stuff that's loud is telling you that you need to do something, you probably don't.

So think about who matters to you and ways that you're able to spend time with them. It might be that on a rough day just sending someone a quick message might feel like a huge step; other days you might feel more able to go out and hang with friends or spend more time with the rest of the family rather than in your room.

Obviously, lots of your social interaction will be online. That's where people tend to hang out. Hopefully you'll also find ways to do some hanging out with another human actually in the room. Connecting with your friends online can be a helpful way to keep in touch, but there is also something special about seeing someone smile when you talk or getting a hug from them.

Have you thought about telling others about your OCD, but been scared to? To open up to others in your life who are on your side and won't judge you (although OCD might tell you that everyone is judging)? This can be a helpful thing to help you feel more connected to others. Find a quiet moment and talk about what OCD is really like. Of course, it's okay to share as little or as much about your OCD as you want to.

Here's some advice for how to tell others about your stuff that's loud:

— Start slow. Everybody feels anxiety sometimes. You might talk about feeling anxious about thoughts that bother you, that you have trouble getting out of your head. You might also talk about how this interferes with stuff in your life—like maybe, your friends feel like you are distant sometimes, or preoccupied. Maybe they've noticed you doing rituals and don't know what to make of them. Starting with things you do, rather than saying "Hey, I have OCD" can help ease people in, and give you time to educate them a bit. Many people don't know what OCD is, or they may have stereotyped ideas about it. Starting slow will help you lay out the details you'd like to share, as they relate to that person and your relationship, at your own pace.

— Share only the details that are important to help others understand and empathize with you. You don't have to share the content of your thoughts unless you want to. However, you could share that you experience thoughts that are scary and hard, and feel shameful or horrible.

— When and if you share with others, don't let the stuff that's loud direct what you say, and how you say it. For example, your stuff that's loud might want you to be sure that you share every single detail, correctly, and to check that it is 100 percent understood. Or perhaps your OCD wants you to tell people so that they accommodate it and make it easier to do OCD rituals. See if you can resist talking about it the way OCD wants you to.

— Stigma busting is scary and hard but can be helpful. Educating others can help remove obstacles for you—and for others. Think about talking to your teachers and friends. Go at your own pace, and choose who you are willing to share with and who you are not.

Another way to reduce stigma is to stand up for yourself when people say, "I'm so OCD." If you've heard someone saying this who *doesn't* have OCD—they just like things neat, or they use hand sanitizer during winter—it can feel offensive. Keep in mind that lots of people just don't understand what it's like. They might say something like "I'm so OCD about my studying," or "I keep my room clean; I'm so OCD." If you are willing to help educate others about OCD, that will make a space for you to feel more comfortable, and it will help others who also have OCD.

Build your army. Connecting with others with OCD can help. There is a whole community out there who understand and want you to join them. The International OCD Foundation website (www.iocdf.org) is a good place to start your search for a community. There are likely to be some local groups near you too.

There is strength in numbers. You can learn from others and offer support to them too. **You are more powerful than you know**. Many of the young people we have worked with are actively involved in helping others—through sharing their experience, through speaking out, through volunteering.

Chapter 10

OTHER STUFF THAT HELPS

Science is clear that a healthy lifestyle can reduce your vulnerability to anxiety or OCD. That doesn't mean it will take away all the stuff that's loud or the urges to quiet those thoughts or feelings. However, when you're feeling stronger, the stuff that's loud is likely to be less frequent and less intense.

SLEEP

Have you noticed that you tend to stay up later and get out of bed later too? That's actually a normal part of adolescence—just when your body needs sleep the most, your body clock makes it hard to sleep at night and be awake in the mornings. It's called a *sleep-phase shift*. This can make it tough to get to school on time; if you are in the habit of late-night video gaming or being on screens, *that* can really make it hard for you to sleep. When your sleep gets messed up, it can increase anxiety and depression. And when you're anxious or depressed, it can be harder to sleep.

So when we tell you that getting enough sleep is likely to help take away some of the power of the stuff that's loud, we are still aware that it might be a challenging thing to work on. If we tell you to get more sleep to help yourself, we have put even more pressure on you to sleep, which might make it harder to sleep. So we're not going to suggest you get more sleep. Instead, we're going to ask you to be curious about how to improve your "sleeportunity."

Sleeportunity is our shorthand way to describe the things you do to help you sleep. Teens should be getting between eight and ten hours of sleep a night, although most young people get less than that. Sometimes you'll sleep for all those hours; other nights you'll be lying in bed hoping to sleep but not able to. Something that helps is to develop what is called *sleep hygiene*, which can help improve how much you sleep, and the quality of your sleep.

Good sleep hygiene includes creating habits. Notice how these practices work for you:

— Go to sleep at the same time each night and be awake in daytime.

— Resist napping.

— If you do stay up later on weekends, still get up at a reasonable time; sleeping in late can mess with your sleep all week.

— Don't have caffeine or energy drinks after 4:00 p.m.

— Avoid alcohol and nicotine.

— Get off your screens a half hour before you want to fall asleep; find something else that relaxes you in the last hour before bed.

— Add more exercise or physical movement into your day.

Also, remember that bodies take a while to get used to a change in sleep routine. If you decide to experiment with a different bedtime or trying different things before bed in order to give yourself more sleeportunity, be aware that you might need to give yourself at least a few weeks of any routine to get enough information about its usefulness. You might want to even keep notes about what helped.

Change doesn't happen overnight …

EXERCISE

We know that exercise can help you feel stronger and give you energy. Exercise also makes your body more tired, which means you might sleep more hours or more deeply, and that will reduce your vulnerability to the stuff that's loud. Exercise can help you feel more willing to take risks and be curious. It also gives you a chance to focus on the here and now—it can be harder to worry about the future when you're just focusing on running to the next lamppost. Some forms of exercise are also social, like team sports, which means you need to get out and spend time with others. Plus there are all sorts of positive physiological and chemical things that happen when you get your body moving.

But if you're like us, you probably find exercise easier said than done. We make all sorts of promises to ourselves and plans that this week we're going to do more, but life gets busy, our bodies get tired, other options feel more appealing at the time, and so on …

So how can you develop an exercise plan that is likely to actually happen? First, pick a type of exercise that appeals to you. Is there a sport you enjoy playing? Are you someone who likes to get out in the sun and go for a run? Perhaps you prefer going to a gym or a pool? Or maybe you like doing exercise in the privacy of your own room—YouTube has lots of great yoga or workout videos to guide you through a workout that's at your level.

It doesn't need to be a whole workout either. Add more small stuff into your day. Walk the dog. Take the stairs instead of the elevator. Get off the bus one stop early and walk to the last stop.

Also be curious about the things that make it more likely that exercise actually happens and the things that discourage you. Can you find a time of day when you actually have time and energy to do it? Can you do the exercise before the game or Netflix comes on? Do you know someone who might enjoy exercising with you? Maybe you can encourage each other? Or sign up for a class or an event?

Bonus points if the exercise you try is also one that allows you to practice your breathing or present-moment focus—examples include yoga or martial arts.

FOOD & DRINK

Are there certain foods or quantities of food that make you feel healthier and better about yourself? Are there other foods that make you feel sluggish or invite your mind to be mean to you? Do your values influence what foods you choose to eat?

There are a million guides to food intake or trendy diets available; some of them might be a good fit for you, helping you feel stronger and more ready to be curious. There are other diets that feed the stuff that's loud, encouraging you to have inflexible rules or complex rituals. So keep your eyes open, and notice whether your chosen diet is allowing you to move toward the life you want to be living, or reinforcing the OCD and social avoidance, or getting in the way of you doing the stuff you care about.

As well as food, there are other substances we can choose to put into our bodies, and again we encourage you to be really curious about what happens. Often getting drunk or wasted on drugs seems like it might allow for a brief break from the stuff that's loud, but it actually makes the stuff that's loud ten times louder the next day when you feel awful and are going over the things you said or did under the influence. Drugs or alcohol are also likely to get in the way of sleep, exercise, and eating patterns that you're choosing to experiment with. Bring your inner scientist, and notice what actual effects these things are having on the life you want to be living.

MEDICATION

If you see a psychiatrist or medical doctor about your OCD, they might recommend medication. Medication is another area where curiosity can be useful. Doctors know a lot about medication and what the research says about effectiveness—so ask lots of questions.

Research on OCD suggests that the skills we describe in this book—specifically, ERP—are your best bet for your OCD. However, some medications have also been shown to help some people with OCD, especially if you use them in addition to ERP. If you think you want to try medication, we suggest you find a doctor who is a good listener and who you feel like you trust. Make sure you feel that you have time to ask any questions you have about the medications and that you're always welcome to go away and think some more before trying anything. You might choose to do your own research, but of course Dr. Google isn't always that reliable, and you'll

find lots of pill lovers and pill haters online, regardless of what the facts actually say. Your OCD will probably not be a reliable source of information either.

You need to be a good listener too. If you try a medication, listen to what your body tells you about whether it's helping or making you feel worse. Give it time to see if the side effects settle. And if you have questions or notice side effects or changes you don't like, call your doctor straightaway. Also, sorry to have to tell you that medication alone won't fix your problems. You might think of it as something that may support your use of the skills in this book.

STEPPING OUTSIDE

If you're like most people in the twenty-first century (including us authors), you probably spend too much time on your devices. Phones, tablets, laptops, TVs, and other screens all compete for our attention and are very skilled at keeping us hooked in and online. They can also keep us disconnected from the world.

What happens when you put down your devices and step outside? What do you notice? Maybe it's just a whole lot of other people walking down the street with their heads down looking at their phones. Or maybe you also notice other things that are happening in the world around you. People, animals, plants, clouds, colors … There's so much to see. So much to connect you to the world that the stuff that's loud is trying to keep you away from.

And while you're outside, or at least away from your screens, what do you enjoy doing? What can you do that will give you a boost? A sport or a hobby or a topic to learn more about? Something that will give you a sense that your world is opening up again or that you have room to move, and that there's so much to discover.

Maybe the stuff that's loud has been causing trouble for so long that you're not even sure what you like. Maybe you'll need to use your curiosity to experiment with different things and find out what you're good at or what you're not yet good at but would like to get better at.

Time is limited. We only have so many hours on this earth. The stuff that's loud wants you to spend every one of those hours doing what it tells you. Now's your chance to spend some of your hours learning more about yourself and what you like to do. Even when the stuff that's loud is trying to stop you. Especially when the stuff that's loud is trying to stop you.

THERAPY

Hopefully the ideas in this book have been helpful for you, and you also might need more support. You might need more support with your OCD, or maybe there are related difficulties, such as alcohol or drug use or past trauma you haven't been able to talk about (or talk enough about).

If you have a diagnosis of OCD, it's important to find a therapist trained in ERP who can guide you well. A great place to do this is to check out the International OCD Foundation website (www.iocdf.org). A good therapist can help you rightsize your ERP and troubleshoot when needed.

You might already be seeing a therapist, or that might be something you want to try. This book draws on principles of acceptance and commitment therapy (ACT), so if it resonates, you might like to try finding a therapist (or counselor or psychologist) who uses ACT so that their ideas and the book's ideas are consistent. Or maybe you want to try someone who works in a different way. Let your curiosity guide you.

Whoever you see, make sure that you feel heard and respected and not just viewed as OCD with legs. You are more than your difficulties. Although your therapist might spend a good bit of time talking about the hard stuff, you still want to feel like they see you as a whole human being. Remember your therapist is a human being too; they haven't got their whole life sorted, and they've got their own thoughts and emotions that cause them distress. And at the same time, maybe they've got some ideas that will help you move closer to the life you want to be living.

EXTRA SUPPORT & IDEAS

As you are finding your way through the stuff that's loud, there's lots of stuff that helps. The International OCD Foundation website (www.iocdf.org) has recommendations, resources, and a whole world of useful ideas. There are books, YouTube clips, podcasts, and discussion groups, and stuff for your family, friends, and teachers too. There's a strong and growing community of young people with OCD who will welcome you—there's an annual conference where you can actually go and meet them! Get curious and discover.

SO LONG FOR NOW, HERE AT THE END...OF THE BEGINNING

We wish you well on your journey. May you have many adventures! May you meet fellow travelers and may you discover, one small step at a time, your many strengths. Our wish for you is that you take the ideas in our little book and build yourself a spectacular life, worthy of all that you are, of all you hope, and all you dream.

Keep the discussion going at:

www.stuffthatsloud.com
or
www.facebook.com/stuffthatsloud.

Spirals grow infinitely small the farther you follow them inward, but they also grow infinitely large the farther you follow them out.

John Green, *Turtles All the Way Down*

ACKNOWLEDGMENTS

Before we go, we have to say a few really important thank-yous.

This book was written after years of talking to young people struggling with OCD, anxiety, sadness, and life. We remember you, we care about you, and we're grateful for all we've learned from you. **Thank you.**

Thank you to the many kids and families struggling with OCD who have been my teachers—you are my heroes. You inspire me, every day, to do my best, just as you do. It's a privilege to walk alongside you on your journeys, and a joy to see you find your many strengths. To Rory, Josie, and John—you are my heart. Thank you for putting up with me, every day. I am not whole without you. To all of the staff at the McLean OCDI Jr.— you amaze me. Without you, we could not make the difference that we do for these many families. I could not love you guys more.

—Lisa

Thank you, kia ora, todah raba to all my amazing family, friends, and community. Geraldine, Susana, Norah, and George—thank you for supporting me, inspiring me, and tolerating me working on this at times when I should have been playing with you. Thank you to all my colleagues at Wellington ACT Centre, Te Aro Psychology and School of Psychology, Victoria University of Wellington, as well as the whole ANZ ACBS community. And a particularly big thank-you to my clients, especially those who have tried ideas from this book. I won't name you here, but I am thinking of you.

—Ben

Huge thank-yous to our many friends and colleagues who have helped, one way or another, as we worked on this project, and especially these folks: Olivier Clarke, Alyssa Faro, Shira Folberg, Ethan Ganster, Evelyn Gould, Louise Hayes, Jialin Hu, Phoebe Moore, Mark Picciotto, Vanessa Sloat, Denise Egan Stack, Jeff Szymanski, Claire Turner, Caitlin White. **Thank you.**

You are our people. We are so grateful to have you in our lives. Thank you with our whole hearts.

Nā tō rourou, nā taku rourouka ora ai te iwi.

With your basket and my basket the people will thrive.

Māori whakataukī (proverb)

Ben Sedley, PhD, is a clinical psychologist and acceptance and commitment therapy (ACT) practitioner with over fifteen years of experience working with adolescents and adults facing mental health difficulties. Sedley's research and practice has focused on examining children and young people's understanding of mental health, which has helped guide him on the best ways to explain mental health concepts and ACT to young people. He is author of the teen self-help book, *Stuff That Sucks*.

Lisa Coyne, PhD, is founder and senior clinical consultant of the McLean OCD Institute for Children and Adolescents (OCDI Jr.), and assistant professor in the department of psychiatry at Harvard Medical School. She also founded and directs the New England Center for OCD and Anxiety, and is coauthor of *The Joy of Parenting* (with Amy Murrell) and *Connect and Shape* (with Koa Whittingham). She lives near Boston, MA, with her family and two therapy dogs, Doog and Peach.

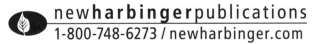